MW00422760

Free!

Eight Graves, Seven Days & One Heart Healed by Love

Copyright © 2015,2018 by Kimberly Joy Krueger
All rights reserved. No part of this book by be used or reproduced in any
manner whatsoever without written permission except the case of brief
quotations embodied in critical articles and reviews and certain other
non-commercial uses permitted by copyright law.

This work is based on the experiences of individuals. Every effort has
been made to ensure the accuracy of the content.

For permission requests, write to the publisher addressed, "Attention:
Permissions Coordinator," at the address below.

FEW International Publications
P.O. Box 271
Mukwonago, WI 53149

Free! Eight Graves, Seven Days, & One Heart Healed by Love
Krueger, Kimberly Joy

Second Edition

Contributing Editor and Interior Layout Design: Reji Laberje,
Independent Consultant of Bucket List To Bookshelf,
www.bucketlisttobookshelf.com, reji.laberje@gmail.com

Cover Design and Interior Layout Graphic Elements: Nada Orlic

All scripture is taken from the New American Standard Bible unless
otherwise noted.

ISBN-13: 978-1949494006
ISBN-10: 1949494004

Categories:
      Biographies & Memoirs > Specific Groups > Women
      Christian Books & Bibles > Christian Living > Death & Grief
      Religion & Spirituality > Worship & Devotion > Faith

Extraordinary Women; Extraordinary Stories
http://kimberlyjoykrueger.com/few.php

This book is dedicated to my children, grandchildren and all future generations. There have been many graves in our family's long and windy wilderness. From this day forward, may our eternal legacy be as grave dancers!

"There is only one happiness in this life, to love and be loved."

~GEORGE SAN

Introduction

I found myself standing in a huge warehouse-like building. It seemed to go on forever in every direction I looked. Everything was pure, stark, hospital-clean, and white. Every single thing was white. I knew it was a heavenly place. I could feel the purity. I quickly noticed that I was in o n e o f m a n y l o n g l i n e s o f people – like at a bank or a g r o c e r y s t o r e check-out lane. In fact, there were many, many lines of people in this endless white warehouse.

I wondered, *'What are we all waiting for?'* No sooner h a d I asked the question, t h e n there was an angel standing at my side.

With a joyful but serious tone he said, "You get to skip."

I was thrilled! As he led me to the front of the line I thought, *'Me? Wow! I get to skip? I wonder why I am so special? And what exactly is it that I am skipping for? Oh, this is so exciting!'*

I felt so loved, special . . . chosen.

FREE!

The closer we got to the front of the line, the more anticipation built up inside me.

I could soon see that every line in this white warehouse was stationed directly in front of a door. As far down to my right as my eye could see were doors with people waiting in front of the doors. I saw the same as I looked to my left. I did not see many people getting to skip ahead like I was doing, though. The angel guided me to stand directly behind the first person in line in front of one of the doors.

I watched as this person went through the door.

My curiosity was not satisfied at all.

I could not see what was on the other side of that mysterious door.

'What am I even skipping ahead to?' I wondered.

My angel guide interrupted my thoughts. "It's your turn."

He took me by the hand and led me to the door. I was elated! I was chosen to skip! I did not have to wait! This was so appealing to my impatient nature. So many were waiting for seemingly so long, but I got to go next!

Another angel opened the door for me and my excitement immediately turned to sheer panic. I looked out, then down, and I saw . . . clouds. Clouds? We were in the sky! We were above the clouds!

Was I supposed to jump?
Yes, I was supposed to jump!
What?
This is what I got to skip for?
No! I was terrified of heights!

Fear clutched my heart as I backed away from the door and said, "No . . . um . . . no, thank you. I don't want to skip."

My angel friend nudged me closer to the door as he reminded me, "You get to skip."

This time I pleaded. "But I don't want to skip anymore!"

He said even more firmly this time, "You do not understand. *You get to skip.*" And with that, he gave me a shove.

I was falling – jumping out of an airplane without a parachute! Can you imagine that type of free fall? Yeah. That. I was in the middle of the sky, falling through the clouds. My stomach was in my throat; every muscle was stiff; I was paralyzed. All breath was lost.

I was falling through levels of panic

to terror

to torment,

when—suddenly—as quickly and completely as the panic had gripped me, it was gone!

I was flying. I was soaring through the air like an eagle! I was diving, and weaving, and laughing! Peace washed over me, joy bubbled up inside me, and FREEDOM surged through me. I was completely renewed in body, soul, and spirit. I was exhilarated.

And then I awoke.

Wide awake.

Eyes wide open.

I felt exhilarated. Even though—at one point—the dream was terrifying, the flying was what stuck with me.

'Wow! I'm special to God. He's letting me skip!'

I didn't know that skipping meant suffering. I didn't understand that is how you skip ahead in His Kingdom. Jesus suffered more than anyone and He also skipped higher than anyone. From suffering straight to the right hand of God. I had no idea that God's way of giving me access to that "door to soar" was to go through eight . . . *graves* – eight "deaths" in my life.

Skipping meant going through . . . Hell.

But I wasn't so quick to pick up on that at the time of the dream. The reality of what the dream meant didn't kick in until I sat down to write this book – after experiencing a one-week healing journey with God. That's when the dots connected. His plans are so obvious in retrospect. That's when they become our ah-ha moments!

His ways are not our ways. He calls us to His healing, His way. God called me on a one-week journey that would set me free when a woman at church introduced me to the Festival of Tabernacles. God used one woman to invite me to my own journey of remembrance. Now I'd like to invite you to join me in those travels through a suffering that allowed me to be able to skip ahead toward our Heavenly Father's Love, a place where we can soar and be truly . . . *FREE!*

The First Grave

The Place Where You Were Abandoned

*"Scars and struggles on the way, but
with joy our hearts can say, yes, our
hearts can say, 'Never once did we ever
walk alone. Never once did You leave us
on our own. You are faithful. God, You
are faithful.'"*

—MATT REDMAN

*I*t was as if I had travelled back in time. Every
one of my five senses was immersed in a
distant memory as I sat in my car, staring at
my childhood home. Although it was dark
outside, as I looked in the windows, I could see my mom,
Leta, my two sisters, and myself in the usual places we
would be found during those dark days. My mom was in
the kitchen, busy doing mom things. Kelly, my older
sister, was upstairs in her room, and Kerrie, my younger

sister, and I were in the family room watching TV. My was not there. I could feel darkness and its persistent presence. The TV only made a feeble attempt to keep it at bay. The darkness lingered, much like a raincloud on a day whose success is hinged on sunshine. Do you know those days? The days when, no matter how hard you wish those clouds away, they seem to multiply?

I hadn't given a name to this darkness when I was living it, but, in a few minutes, while sitting in my car with pen and journal in hand, I would. I would name it to be able to expel it. In the meantime, I could taste the anger. If you've ever tasted anger, you know it tastes bitter. Very bitter. If you haven't, then I am genuinely glad for you! I tasted anger now and it seemed to get worse when mixed with the fear I felt as I heard yelling and crying from inside the house. There was no way to spit this taste out of my mouth.

In an effort to get my mind off of the anger and fear, I steered it back to that cloud. What was that looming darkness? I lived so many years wrapped in it but couldn't put my finger on it. It had to do with loneliness, yet loneliness didn't fully describe it. It was much more like aloneness. It had nothing to do with how many people were present. It was abandonment's sting. I looked at my house and my neighborhood with an ache that, I guess, followed me from the time I was seven years old. I pitied us. Each one of us.

I pitied my mom, for having to do it alone.

I pitied Kelly for having to grow up way too fast.

I pitied Kerrie for being so little and so deeply wounded that she couldn't sleep alone for the first three years after Dad left.

And I pitied me for falling for the enemy's bitter trap – hook, line, and sinker.

Then, as I sat in my car, I turned and saw Him at the end of our road. Only one or two streetlights lit the road between us. As He rounded the corner of my street, I recognized Him.

It was Jesus.

His sparkling, beautiful eyes were full of love and fixed, determinedly, on my house. His pace was steady and swift. His spotless white robe flowed gracefully with each step and He didn't miss a beat as He made His way toward my house. I heard the crunch of the gravel beneath His sandals as He walked up my driveway. He turned onto to the walkway, past the shrubs, and walked right up to the front door. He raised His hand and knocked.

No answer.

He waited.

He knocked again.

Still no answer.

He knocked more firmly. I could feel His incredible patience as He waited for someone to answer the door. As He repeated this process I held my breath waiting for someone to answer.

'Answer!' I yelled in my mind, *'Someone answer the door! It's Jesus! And you all need Him – DESPERATELY!'* But no one did.

FREE!

Then I saw myself walking toward the front door! *'Oh, thank God!' I thought.*

But I continued right past the door and up the stairs, as if I had no idea anyone was there. My heart was broken!

Why didn't I hear Him knock?

It is the next scene that released a flood of tears as I sat there, parked in front of my childhood home, engrossed this gut-wrenching scene as it unfolded.

After waiting patiently, Jesus began to circle my house, stopping at each and every window in an attempt to get our attention. He stood at the family room window looking longingly at my sister as she watched TV. He stood there for quite a while attempting to get her attention. Were we ignoring Him or just oblivious to His Presence? My heart felt sick!

He stopped at every window hoping to catch our eye so that we could see the Love in His. He pressed His face up against the glass, peering, lifting His Hand at times to get our attention. I felt His longing. He ached to be let in. Suddenly, I was saddened and grieved by His pain instead of ours.

After many attempts, He slowly turned around, left our yard and walked back down my street. Through my tear streaked eyes, I saw Him turn the corner where the road ends, until He was no longer in sight. All I could think about was how He must have felt.

I cried out, "Lord! Why didn't we answer? I'm so sorry I didn't answer!"

My tender, merciful, perfect Lord replied, "It's okay. You couldn't hear. It's hard to hear my still, small voice over the angry voices. But I came for you. Every day. I kept coming for you. I kept knocking until you let me in."

Overwhelmed with His Presence and the love that this vision filled me with, I wondered, 'Wow, this is surreal! How did I even end up here tonight?'

Lost in the moment I was having with Him, I had briefly forgotten the reason I was parked in front of my childhood home....

You know you are in the midst of a moment of destiny when God Himself interrupts your life and tells you to do something kind of crazy.

That's exactly what He did to me.

Two days before setting out for my childhood home, I experienced a Divine Intervention.

I could have easily dismissed it as my own imagination, but it was far too great and detailed for me to come up with on my own. I'm just not that creative!

THE LORD INVITED ME ON A JOURNEY OF REMEMBRANCE.

The Lord invited me on a journey of remembrance with Him. He led me to revisit what He called the "graves" of my past. These graves were places that represented great loss and pain – places of sorrow and mourning that He was now promising to turn into joy and dancing. Some were figurative graves and some literal. I was sure it wasn't my idea, because—as exciting as the dancing part was to me—no one looks forward to visiting a grave, even if it is a figurative one! He was inviting me to a deeper healing and, just like the Creator would, He crafted this pilgrimage quite uniquely.

After church services on Wednesday, September 22, 2010, a friend came up to me and said, "Kim! Did you know that tonight is the first night of the Festival of Tabernacles? Here! You should read this!"

I found myself standing alone with a small stack of printouts and a strong feeling that I should, indeed, read them. I read of this Jewish Feast in the Old Testament many times (a feast that God required Israel to celebrate each year), but I never understood its purpose. With a sense of urgency, I went home, got my kids to bed, and began reading.

I learned that the Festival of Tabernacles, also known as the Feast of Sukkot, was a seven day remberance of the forty years the Israelites spent in the wilderness. The way they were to remember and celebrate what God had done for them was to set up tents (also called tabernacles) like those in which their ancestors lived during their forty year journey to The Promised Land.

This exercise served two purposes: the first was to remind them that the wandering was temporary. The Wilderness was a route to The Promised Land . . . not intended to be their final destination. Secondly, they were to rejoice in all the ways God was faithful to them during those forty years.

And His faithfulness to them was boundless!

It was in the wilderness that God chose to introduce the many facets of His nature to them. It was there that they met God as their Protector, Healer, Provider, and Guide. Manna, food from Heaven, appeared supernaturally every day, keeping them fed for forty years.

He protected them from the heat of the day with the cloud and from the cold of night with the pillar of fire. He saw to it that their shoes and clothing did not wear out for forty years, while simultaneously keeping them safe from their enemies. He healed them from diseases and forgave their stubborn rebellion, over and over and over again. He even brought forth water from a rock when they were thirsty. And we musn't forget how they arrive in the Wilderness to begin with! He freed them from four hundred years of brutal slavery by a merciless Pharaoh with the parting of The Red Sea!

The Feast of Sukkot isn't just a call to intentionally remember of all of these mighty works of God, but a call to remember who God was to them. On the eighth day, the feast culminates in celebration as they put away their tents and return to the homes the Lord blessed them with in the Land of Promise. They are to rejoice because the God of the temporary Wilderness is also the Faithful God who leads His people into their Land of Promise to dwell permanently.

As I read about this beautiful custom, the Lord was moving my heart. He wanted me to remember, not just what He did for the children of Israel, but what he did for this child . . . for me. As my Good Shepherd, God reminded me of my own personal wilderness. My past was much like the wilderness wanderings of Israel; long, dry, and seemingly unending. Like them, I felt unsafe and insecure and encountered much suffering. And like them, I discovered many of the facets of God's merciful character.

God brought water from a rock for me, too. This time, the rock was my heart and the water? His Spirit. He faithfully fed them manna, and me? The bread of His Word.

Through all the brokenness and loss, He kept me warm, as He did for the Israelites with the fire. He clothed me for protection, as the cloud protected His Jewish people. He never left my side.

I was reminded of Psalm 30:11, a verse I stumbled across at least three times during the week prior to the Festival of Tabernacles:

You have turned for me, my mourning into dancing.

It was all starting to make some sense to me! God was taking me back to those painful days to heal me. I went to bed, after reading about the Feast of Tabernacles, with a spirit of hope and expectation. I knew something incredible was about to happen; I couldn't wait to see what tomorrow would bring.

By lunchtime the next day, His plan was crystal clear. I was talking on the telephone with Lynda, one of my spiritual mothers. I was processing all that I had learned the night before and what was stirring in my heart. I told her I was sure that I was being called to a spiritual journey. That is when it became clear that I would take a physical journey to specific places in my past. They were places on a map that may not mean much to most people, but to me represented sorrow, suffering, and great loss. According to Psalm 30:11, the places where I once mourned would somehow be turned into places of joy.

It was safe to assume joy would come because who dances without joy? Have you ever tried to dance when you were grieving? You simply can't; you're too broken. That meant my brokenness would have to be healed! I wasn't sure how He'd pull this one off, but I knew I would only find out if I obeyed.

> IT WAS SAFE TO ASSUME JOY WOULD COME BECAUSE WHO WOULD DANCE WITHOUT JOY?

"I think God wants you to go to the actual places from your past, Kim!" Lynda's voice had a sense of urgency and excitement when she told me this. The Holy Spirit bore witness in my heart and I knew she was right.

"Yes! You're right! I am!" As we hung up, I wondered where exactly I would be going with God over the next week. Memories flooded my mind. There were so many places to choose from, but I knew I wasn't the one who should be choosing. I grabbed pen and paper and sat down at my kitchen table. I was ready to listen.

"What are the graves, Lord? Where do you want me to go?" I asked.

At this point, I didn't even know how many there would be, much less where they would be located, but He answered quickly. Honestly, I think it took me all of two minutes to write down the "stops" I would make over the next week. They flowed from my hand to that pad of paper with more ease than any other to-do-list I had ever written. Once I had them all down, He told me to number them according to the order that they happened. He then gave each one a name. They are the names of the graves listed in this book. I have not changed them as I was not the one to title them. He is the author.

There were eight graves in all: two literal graves and six figurative ones. I sat for a moment and stared at the sum of my life's pain listed on the same paper I used to make my grocery lists.

He spoke. "It is time for you to remember your wanderings and to rejoice in My faithfulness to you. You are to recount all that I have done for you because soon you will cross over into your own Promised Land."

Promised Land? Really? The place I never thought I would get to? Since I was thirty-nine years old, this meant that I would enter my personal Land of Promise the same year I turned forty! A forty-year journey, just like the children of Israel! The same God who was faithful to them, was faithful to me, too. Wow. It was too remarkable and well-conceived to be my idea.

My instructions and map were complete.

My own personal Festival of Tabernacles had started.

I had a journey to take.

I wrote all that happened in my journal. I collected and saved articles on the Festival of Tabernacles. I knew that I was about to be changed forever and I wanted to understand as much as I could. The how wasn't so clear yet, but the why and the when sure were. I guess the how didn't really matter, because He was telling me these places, memories, and events would no longer be a source of pain to me. They would become a source of joy and even, dare I think, cause for dancing. I was absolutely sure of this: He was not going to fail me. He never had before.

I said, "Yes!" and began to mentally chart out my journey. It was time to go "grave-dancing."

That is what brought me to grave number one on the very next day, a mere thirty-six hours after God had sent me to church on that Wednesday night.

**This was my childhood home;
the place where I was abandoned.**

My stomach tingled with a nervous, excited feeling when I drove slowly down my old street. I wasn't sure what was about to happen, but I expected it to be good . . . especially this particular grave, because I was over it . . . or so I thought.

My initial reaction upon arrival was probably pretty typical. The trees looked huge and the yards looked tiny! Our family home had received a makeover, but it was definitely the same one. I wondered how many of our old neighbors still lived here. I gazed for a while at the tree my dad had planted in the center of the front yard. It all seemed like a million years ago that my parents had the fight that inspired my dad to plant that tree. As I sat in front of my old house, dealing with the emotions and reactions one would expect, I settled my mind to wait on the Lord to reveal His agenda for the night. I closed my eyes and sat quietly in my car with my journal, pen, and tissue next to me, marveling at this journey I was on.

I began to see and feel memories flooding in. Some of them were good, but I noticed quickly that I was fixated on all the bad ones:

Thoughts of the night when I was seven years old and my dad told us he was leaving consumed me. I remembered how my mom and my older sister cried all night. I remembered wondering why they were so upset when he promised that he was coming back. He traveled frequently and he always came back! Why was everyone so upset? Then I remembered how I felt when I finally figured out that he wasn't coming back.

All at once, the heavy, dark feeling of aloneness settled over me. I felt the fear and the emptiness all over again, like it was fresh. I began to weep. I carried that lonely feeling around for so many years. Sometimes, even in a room full of people, it consumed my soul.

I remembered how, up until the day he left, I had never worried about what I would eat, or if I would have clothes and enough of the things I needed. I thought of the stark contrast between the Christmases before and after the divorce. I felt the embarrassment that I carried with me on the first days of school when I was wearing last year's clothes and shoes. My new life was marked by poverty, powerlessness, and anger. Underneath it all was one haunting question:

Why wasn't I worth fighting for?

Eventually, my life reflected the belief I adopted: that I wasn't. I wasn't worth it. I lived as if it were a fact, although it was never rooted in the truth. Heck, sometimes I felt like I wasn't even worth seeing, much less loving. I became an angry child and an even angrier teen as I realized that security was only a memory from the earliest days of my childhood. It didn't help that I hardly ever saw my dad after the separation.

Once, in an act of desperation, my sister Kelly and I took one of my mom and dad's wedding pictures and cut it into little puzzle pieces. We carefully cut around my dad's face and set it aside. Then we put all of the other pieces into an envelope addressed to my dad with a note that read: "Dad, put this puzzle together and find the missing piece."

I was crushed when he left. By the time I was ten years old, I told my dad that I hated him and that I never wanted to see him again. Of course, this was not true, but I was in pain and there is no better arsenal of protection against pain than some good old-fashioned anger.

The end of my parents' marriage and family life as I knew it was much like having the ultimate rug pulled out from under me. After that I learned to wait for the next rug to go, too. One day, we were a typical upper middle-class family. We had a new car every two years, vacation every year, and house in the suburbs. The next moment, I was the daughter of a single mother who was waitressing to make ends meet, living in a house that was falling apart. The house was a rude physical reminder of our emotional reality. Not only did we have no vacations or new cars, but we didn't even always have groceries in the cabinet. I was pissed. I was mad that my dad's lifestyle didn't change, but ours did.

Sadly, though, my dad wasn't the only recipient of my anger. I was angry with my mom, too, although I couldn't identify why until I was an adult. In hindsight, I can plainly see that, in a different way, she left me, too. Not because she wanted to, but because she needed to. She had to leave her role as a stay-at-home mom and get a full-time job to support us. On top of that, she was emotionally crushed when her marriage ended; she didn't want the divorce. She was a casualty trying to help three other casualties. This became easy for me to understand after my own divorce many years later, nevertheless, an abandoned child is completely incapable of understanding anything other than this – I am alone now. I am afraid.

> I AM ALONE NOW. I AM AFRAID.

I attempted to quell my fear and fill my loneliness in multiple ways. I started drinking and smoking in seventh grade, at twelve years old. That quickly led to getting high at the age of thirteen. Pot, pills, alcohol, and cigarettes were my daily life.

Of course, I did all of this behind my parents' back under the guise of "it's just fun!" I didn't know I was trying to fill a hole. I was just trying to FEEL something.

Another secret I hid from everyone was an eating disorder. When that hole isn't filled, you begin to think that the way you look could change the way you feel. It started at age thirteen in a very innocent way. I was in the bathroom at school when my best friend came in. Like typical middle-schoolers, we struggled with body image, comparing ourselves to the ultra-thin supermodels (in our eyes) in the school.

"Did you know that you can eat and not gain weight if you just throw up after you eat?" she suggested.

I thought it was awesome. I had no idea that her "helpful tip" would lead to thirteen years of binging and purging, an even worse identity problem, obsessive compulsive eating, decades of body image struggles, and a love/hate relationship with food. I would be into adulthood, as a mother of two, before I would even reveal that secret to my mom and sisters.

As a teen though, I went from an honor roll student to barely passing.

I went from content to entitled, believing everybody owed me something.

I went from a typical teen to an angry, rebellious, hostile force in my home.

I would later find out that guests to our house were given a "warning talk" about how I might behave when they visited.

Sitting in my car that night, I realized that all of these memories had been in black and white. Maybe because it was dark out or maybe because abandonment and self-destruction don't come in Technicolor®. I don't know. I couldn't fathom where this joy promised to me was going to come from. What really bothered me was that, up until then, I thought I was pretty much over this!

The pain overwhelmed me and I finally said, "Okay, Lord. I guess I knew this was a grave. No argument there, but where is the joy? What's the cause for celebration?"

His answer was that heart-melting vision of Him walking up to my house and coming for us.

His words? "I came for you. Every day. I kept coming for you. I kept knocking until you let me in."

The answer echoed in my ears and I was a puddle.

My paradigm completely shifted. I was never alone; I only believed I was. It was easy to believe, because anger is a lonely place. And He was right. Anger is so loud that it's hard to hear anything else. After He showed me what was going on all of those years, and I pictured Him coming for me every day, I knew that He was always with me. The place that had represented being unwanted and unloved became a symbol of the most beautiful expression of unconditional love I had ever experienced.

He loved me.
He wanted me.
He came for me.
He never stopped coming.

I sat in my car with half of the box of tissues in a soggy, crumpled pile, thanking Him for being that kind of God – the kind that never leaves, never forsakes. I felt the heaviness begin to lift. Then, like popcorn, good thoughts and memories began to explode in my mind, one after another.

I began to remember the events that took place in my life, not in spite of my father's leaving, but because of it. I am here to tell you that thankfulness is a lens you can choose to put on and see life from a whole new perspective. After I saw the Love of God that came for me every day, my heart was full of gratitude. It was precisely then that the lenses dropped over my eyes and I saw all of the good that had escaped my vision for so many years.

It was always there; it was just buried under self-pity. Not anymore. The memories of good flooded out every dark cloud, every lonely tear. I realized for the first time what a gift my life had been! Instead of viewing my childhood through a victim's lens, I now looked back and saw a childhood of privilege.

Yes, privilege.

What the enemy meant for my harm, God used for good! Every brick thrown at me, My Lord laid down as a path that led me right here, right now. He even used some of those bricks as cornerstones for my future calling.

The most precious gift I received in that place was the gift of salvation. It may have been a gravesite for my parent's marriage, but it was my spiritual birthplace! This was the place where my mom taught me about Jesus. She read us Bible stories, took us to church, and made sure we were saved. Then, after my parents separated, my mom began to hold prayer meetings in our living room. It was there that I was filled with the Holy Spirit. My mom baptized me in our bathtub. I experienced the Presence of God in that house and that same Presence of God beckoned me back to Him after my angry, rebellious years.

No matter how broken my mother was, she left an indelible spiritual imprint on all three of her daughters. I thought of the many abandoned children who never heard about God, much less had Him living inside them. I was blessed! He was not only with me all along, He was in me.

All of a sudden, I found myself having some kind of Back to the Future moment. Do you remember that part in the movie where Marty McFly realizes that, when he tampered with the past, it totally altered the future? That's exactly what happened to me! I began to see two pivotal events that took place during my teenage rebellion that I wouldn't want to change for a single minute, for it would have completley robbed me of so much blessing. These events would not have happened without my parents' divorce. That sure put some things into perspective!

The first happened when I was ten years old and I wouldn't trade it for anything! My mom met Louie and Lisa, some of the dearest people I've ever known, when she went back to work as a single mom. If Mom had not been forced to work because of the separation, she never would have met them. This friendship, which began as my mom's, quickly transferred to me and is still a rock in my life to this day. Louie was a consultant to the owner of the restaurant where my mom worked and Lisa, a cook. My mom and Lisa became fast friends and our families began to do everything together.

Louie stepped in as a father figure to my sisters and me. Eventually, Louie and Lisa offered each of us girls work in their catering business. It was there that I learned everything I needed to know about surviving in the real world. They taught me respect and they taught me to work hard . . . really hard. I worked twelve straight hours without a break on my first day of catering.

When Joseph was a slave and prisoner in Egypt, he had no idea that he was being prepared for a much larger task.

I had no idea that catering for ten years was God's way of preparing me to become a mother to twelve children!

Eventually, Lisa and Louie gave me opportunities in their company that I didn't even think I could handle. They knew I could and they believed in me. They encouraged me frequently, despite the fact that Lisa now describes me as having had a lot of grit. (That was her nice way of saying I was a total brat.) Nevertheless, they patiently taught me and, under their leadership, in many ways, I blossomed into a confident and capable young woman.

Later, when I was an adult with a growing family, Lisa and I became inseparable. We raised our children together, laughed together, and served the Lord together. We have walked our journeys together for thirty-plus years now! Louie and Lisa were a huge gift to me when I needed them most and they still are. I couldn't see it as a child, not even as a teenager, but now I could fill this book with the goodness they have shown to me and my family. I treasured my thoughts and memories of them.

Next, I found myself laughing out loud, remembering, "Kim! Duh! This is where you lived when you gave birth to your son! Now that's cause for rejoicing!"

I was not sure how I could allow anything to overshadow that fact. I immediately concluded that all was worth it to hold Jesse's precious life in my hands.

Finding out I was pregnant at sixteen was shocking, but I knew that I was going to love that baby with everything I had and that being a mother was my calling. As I remembered this monumental event, I saw myself as that rebellious sixteen-year old I had become, with braces, big eighties hair, and all, holding my newborn baby in my arms. I could almost smell that newborn smell as I remembered the hours I spent holding and kissing Jesse. The joy of motherhood bubbled up inside me all over again. I saw the beacon of light that he brought into the darkened world I was living in at that time. And not just mine . . . but all of our lives.

He was pure joy to my mom, who always wanted a son, and to both of my sisters, too. I recalled how his life surely saved mine, as he gave me a reason to live. During my teen years, I walked away from my faith and jumped on a destructive path.

"I don't care what happens to me," were the words I lived by. That is, until I looked into Jesse's perfect eyes. I immediately determined that "I do care what happens to him, though."

My life would never be the same.

It was because of Jesse that I would return to my faith. I wanted more for him than I was living, so I raised the bar. I began to make good choices . . . much better choices. His life saved mine! I don't know if I'd be here today if it were not for him. I wept and thanked God for the gift of life that came in more ways than one in the form of my son.

FREE!

In contrast to my hardness of heart as a youth, my heart flooded with warmth as I thought of my dear dad. He had no idea that his choices would lead to such things for his three girls and he certainly didn't mean for me to question my worth! He loved me, always has loved me, and I could feel the warmth of his love. And oh, how I love him now!

I always did, but my bitterness and fear of not being worth fighting for proved to be such a roadblock to that love and even more of a roadblock to receiving his love in return. By the time I found myself at this profound gravesite, that roadblock had been obliterated for years.

TRUTH is what crashed through that roadblock. The truth of who I am in Christ.

If a perfect God thinks I am worthy of Love, which He does, then my worth and my security cannot be shaken by any person.

Lynda, my spiritual mom and mentor, always says that the truth trumps the facts. Fact: I was left and I felt alone. That is indeed a fact. The truth is I was never alone. His Word tells me so; His heart showed me so; that is the Rock I stand on today. That is the strength I live with, love with, and am loved because of. I was freed to love my mom and dad, regardless of the past, the way God loves me. After all, where would I be if the Father's love for me was conditional? I shudder to think. I marvel at how free I am from the prison of self-pity, anger, and bitterness that held me for so long and how Love, Himself, has made me into His secure daughter.

And oh, I rejoice!

The last cause for celebration at this grave was not like the others. With a heart full of gratitude for all of the kindness God showed to me during this hot and dry wilderness, I began to receive a new revelation. After having spent years as a victim of my parents, I saw it very differently now.

My father and mother did not make me an angry, bitter child. Their choices only revealed my tendency to become angry and bitter. They did not force me to rebel, party, violate laws and rules, and become a teen mom. That is how my heart responded to the circumstances. Those were choices I made . . . choices that hurt me and hurt them, by the way. My parents have three daughters, but not all three daughters became angry, bitter, and rebellious.

Our circumstances are a filter that God can use to separate the good from the bad in each of our hearts and that is exactly how He used mine. My parents' ugliness simply revealed mine. As I understood this new concept, I immediately thanked Him for the gift of wisdom and understanding. My prayer of thanks sang out in my heart:

"Lord, thank you for allowing my circumstances to reveal the sin in my heart—my tendency to become angry, bitter and rebellious. Through these circumstances in my childhood, You allowed me to come face to face with my own brokenness. And ulitmately, it was the desperation in my own heart that led me to You. Thank you for showing me my deep need for You!"

The Bible teaches us that all have sinned and fall short of the glory of God. (Romans 3:23) We all have sinful hearts. Mine was a selfish, angry one. I say "was" because I have a new heart now. So can you. The great news is that, whatever your life has revealed about your heart, whether it's angry like mine, or fearful, or jealous, or bitter, you are promised a new one!

Here's what I can tell you for sure: God won't give you a new heart if you don't ask him to do so. How will you know to ask for one if you never see how badly you need it? Since He already knows what lies in the heart of every man and woman (and wants so much to set each one FREE), could it be His mercy that allows our circumstances to reveal our hearts to us? He knows that there is nothing more dangerous to the human heart than thinking: 'I'm just fine how I am.' That is called denial! Denial will put you in a prison, while making you think you are living in a penthouse. Our God is all about waking His children up so He can take them from the prison to the penthouse!

With no more reason to be angry or to feel sorry for myself, I found myself thankful for my family's story. I know; it sounds contradictory to be thankful for such a mess, but God turned our ashes into beauty! Once you have the beauty, you don't mind the ashes so much.

God's "Plan A" in the garden was his "no ashes plan." Adam and Eve kind of blew that out of the water, so "Plan B" was to send His Son, Jesus, to make it possible for every ash . . . even the ashes of a broken home . . . to be turned into something beautiful.

Now that is cause for dancing!

The goodness of God washed over me in waves. He melted my heart that night by showing me how He came for me every day. He used others to reach me and love me when I couldn't hear His voice. He found a way to draw out the good in me that had been buried under that hardened heart. His Spirit never left me and, best of all, He blessed me with a son! He did so, regardless of the lifestyle I was living.

He restored my relationships with both my mother and my father and showed me how to love them and to feel loved by them. I rejoiced for that and, ultimately, for knowing God and having a relationship with Him. I thanked Him and believed that this grave had lost its sting. I cried cleansing tears as His Spirit refreshed and renewed my heart. I sensed that we were finished here, so I fished around in the dark for my journal and pen, jotted down my new perspectives on this very old grave, and then headed for home.

One down, seven more to go.

FREE!

The Second Grave

The Place Where You Were Abused

*Yes, let none who trust and wait hopefully
and look for You be put to shame or be
disappointed; let them be ashamed who
forsake the right or deal treacherously
without cause.*

—PSALM 25:3 AMPC

*"A wise woman wishes to be no one's
enemy; a wise woman refuses to be
anyone's victim."*

—MAYA ANGELOU

*I*t was day four of my one week pilgrimage, late afternoon on a Sunday. Since it was still light out, I could see every detail of this house. As I studied the colors of this house, the landscape, and the garage, I noticed that not much had changed at all and I didn't like the way that made me feel. Coming back here made me very uncomfortable as an ick-feeling settled on me. I looked at each window and recalled the rooms and corresponding memories that hid behind them.

The memories in my mind were like flashes of a camera—leaving me stunned and seeing white spots for a moment. I gave that house an incredulous glare.

How could I have allowed it to happen?

What was I thinking?

How could I be so stupid?

I was only fifteen when I met Tony and, being honest, I didn't even like him. In fact, he annoyed me because he wouldn't leave me alone. He would ask me question after question while flirting with me.

"What's your name?"

"What are you doing this weekend?"

"What's your phone number?"

He was persistent to say the least. After several weeks, he wore me down and I finally gave him my number. He asked me to come over to his house and cut his hair, so I agreed to talk about it over the phone.

Somehow, that phone call led to another, which led to a car ride. All of this led to us being joined at the hip in short order. What exactly caused me to suddenly be joined at the hip with someone I had recently dismissed as annoying? That's easy . . . his words. He said all the right things. He said that I was beautiful, smart, and talented. He said he wanted to be with me or talking to me all the time. He told me he loved me and that he couldn't live without me. I finally felt wanted. Valuable. Not alone. Worth fighting for.

I FINALLY FELT WANTED. VALUABLE.

At the time of Tony entering my life, I was dried out and hardened, like an old sponge that sat under the sink for years. Although I was loved, I felt so unloved. At this point, I had already been numbing my pain with drugs and alcohol for three years. Now, I lapped up his "love" like a thirsty dog. Being Hell-bent on self-destruction made me a professional at using my worst judgement. It seemed that the more terrible an idea was for my future, the more I liked it. And with his words, this dried out sponge was being run under water for the first time in years.

At first, the water ran right over and off of me, but with a squeeze here and a squeeze there, this sponge finally soaked it up! Every drop. Soon, I couldn't get enough. This sponge had a seemingly unlimited ability to absorb it all and I was only happy when all of these loving words were flowing like the water from the faucet. The water supply stayed steady just long enough for me to be totally hooked, just how he wanted it. Then one day, he turned the faucet off. Well, I guess he didn't turn it off completely. He just changed it. Instead of pleasant and soothing warm water, it was suddenly freezing cold. Instead of hearing about how wonderful I was, I found myself listening to the most cruel, hateful, abusive words coming through the phone.

I was useless to him, and he was done with me. I was a liar, a fake, and not to be trusted. My initial reaction was shock and confusion.

'Wait! What?'

I thought He said I was beautiful, sweet, and funny. What happened? He said he couldn't live without me. How in the world was it so easy for him to just discard me altogether? No! This couldn't be! This could not be confirmation that I wasn't worthy of love! It could not be that no one who got close to me would fight for me or even stick around! At this, the confusion and sting of his words were replaced with fear, panic, and desperation.

I was desperate to know what I had to do or say to turn that warm water back on. I could not take any more cold water. I'd do anything to get that feeling back. I didn't want to dry up again! My internal dialogue was frighteningly close to that of a crack addict plotting out how she would get her next fix.

> MY INTERNAL DIALOGUE WAS FRIGHTENINGLY CLOSE TO THAT OF A CRACK ADDICT.

I began apologizing to him for whatever I did to make him so angry. Although I hadn't actually done anything I was accused of, he wasn't going to be easily swayed. So, I began to plead with him.

"Please! I'm sorry! Please forgive me so we can get back to how things were."

Eventually, he agreed to take me back . . . reluctantly. What a relief! Yes, I was relieved to be placing my heart back into the hands of someone who clearly had no interest in taking care of it. This same scene, with differing details, would go on to play out again and again. Each time with increasing intensity and each time with him growing more powerful in the relationship and me giving more of myself away: time, money, sex, freedom . . . whatever I had to give away in order to get more of his "love." Eventually, our back and forth power struggles (him gaining and me relinquishing) escalated until they became physically abusive.

Tony's anger always came out of nowhere. The reasons for it were never the same, but one thing was consistent: it was my fault. It was always my fault. He attacked me verbally and emotionally first, then he'd move on to physical fighting. I always apologized to try to get it to stop. It didn't work.

After some time in the tumultuous relationship, I found myself pregnant. After all, our typical night was "Netflix and Chill" before there really was such a thing.

It was about eight months after I started dating Tony that I took the pregnancy test in:

My second grave;
the place where I was abused.

I was going to be a mother. And he would be…a father? My mind swirled. I was scared, nervous and excited.

Excited? Yes! I loved babies! My sisters actually called me a baby hog. If there was a baby within a one-mile radius, I had to be holding it. I had it in my heart from the time I was a little girl that I wanted a big family but starting so young certainly wasn't part of the plan. I knew I would keep my baby, but I had no idea how to tell my mom and dad. They were going to be so mad. And as for how I would raise a child while I was a still child? I had no idea. I was a teen mom with braces and big eighties hair believing it would all just "work out."

I was about four months along when yet another of my and Tony's fights started. We were standing in the kitchen getting a snack . . . Doritos or something. It was a cold, dark, winter night and being a Saturday, nobody else was home. The TV was on in background; it always was – Love Boat or Fantasy Island – something; I'm not sure. Pre-pregnancy, this would have been a party night for us. Now our parties were just him and I: sometimes a video rental and almost always messing around. As I stood there fueling up in the kitchen, Tony began to accuse me of flirting with other guys and it only escalated from there.

Tony would routinely accuse me of, well, everything (with other guys). It would start as a simple, *'I saw you look at him,'* and move to, *'You're sleeping with him!'* in moments.

As if I would go from a glance to physical intimacy in a second! I never gave him reason to mistrust me, but he did it to feel powerful, in control of me, and to hear me beg for mercy. I typically would reassure him of my undying loyalty to him. I would do whatever I had to do to calm him down. I wouldn't stick up for myself much.

'I didn't sleep with him, but I shouldn't have even looked at him. I'm so sorry.' I'd say whatever I had to say to appease him without implying guilt.

If he would back down verbally and in his body language, I'd know I was successful in quelling the storm. The tension would hang in the air a bit and he'd warn me I better keep it that way, but the threat would fade. I would be the one who moved us back into affection after that, nudging my way back into his arms.

Instead of pleading for his trust or begging forgiveness for things I hadn't done, this time, I stood my ground. This time, I defended myself. This time, I talked back.

"Screw you! I didn't do any of those things!"

He was indignant, in shock that I actually yelled back. RAGE took over his face and body as I watched his fists clench and back straighten. Tony was six foot two and thin, but strong. His eyes would turn to slits when he was angry. His teeth would grit. His voice would change. He'd lunge toward me, towering over me, in order to intimidate me. He'd set the stage with his tone and body language, even getting shaky before he'd get ready to raise a hand to me.

I looked at him this time and knew, 'Oh my God. I have to run.'

I ran through the foyer, up the stairs. Thirteen stairs. I was on my way to bad luck. I used to dream, as a child, that I could jump from the top to the bottom in a single leap. Instead, I was going up wishing I could do that in one step. I skipped the stairs, a couple at a time. I don't know how he didn't catch me. I wasn't a fast runner, but that 'fight or flight' surge of adrenaline was really helping.

At the top of the stairs, was my bedroom. I didn't really know where I was running. I ran into my walk-in closet, pulled the wooden slatted door closed and tried to hold it. Seriously, my mind was a wash. Do you know those horror movies where you yell at the girl on the screen NOT to go where she'll be trapped? I get it! But that is exactly what I did. The thought of going out of the house or knocking on a neighbor's door hadn't even occurred to me. My mind just said run. It didn't say where to.

I saw him through the slats before he made his way to me. Tony easily pulled the closet door open from the outside. He reached into the door, grabbed me by the hair, and took me down to my closet floor. Still pulling my hear, he slammed my head into the floor three times as he spit out expletives.

"Stop you're hurting me! Stop you're hurting me!" I screamed.

He was full of fury.

I was full of terror.

At some point, I remember physically pushing back. I wasn't fighting to attack, but to free myself to get away. Somehow, I crawled out from under him and made my way toward the stairs. He was right behind me, grabbed me, and then pushed me down the stairs. There was a landing before the final two stairs made a ninety degree turn to the main level. I tumbled down eleven stairs and rolled up against the wall on the landing.

I somehow uttered the words, 'I can't believe you pushed me down the stairs. I'm pregnant with your baby!'

Every movie I've ever seen with a woman losing a baby was because of her being pushed down the stairs.

He said, "Oh my God! What did I just do?"

His finally going "too far," sobered him up. He had been drunk with rage, me with fear. Our focus was now not on us, but on the child. We calmed down. I don't remember getting up, only that I did and told him to stay away from me. But it did not take long for everything became "normal" for us again. He was sorry and suddenly really nice . . . for a little while. After all, we were in love. (Or so I thought.)

Despite my secret abusive relationship, I actually did make great strides toward growing up while I was pregnant, much to my own surprise. I worked as many hours catering as I could and managed to save over one thousand dollars in the short time between finding out I was pregnant and giving birth. I got my GPA up from a 2.1 to a 3.8. I began to prepare for my baby, and I was excited. It was three weeks before Jesse was born that

FREE!

Tony punched me in the face and I began to wake up. He hit me because I wouldn't take the thousand dollars I'd been saving for our child out of my bank account to bail him out of some legal trouble. I was slowly coming out of a deep sleep. That undeserved punch was like one of those slaps to the face that are given out in movies when a friend is shouting, *'Get it together!'*

My final wakeup call happened at 3:20 a.m., when I held Jesse in my arms for the first time. Jesse J. was born on Saturday, July 2, 1988, two weeks before my seventeenth birthday.

When I held that helpless, precious little life in my own hands, I knew I was the only person in the world who would protect him. I knew I had to end my relationship with his father.

What had been good enough for me was just not good enough for my son! I still didn't care that much about myself, but Jesse was another story. I ended the relationship when Jesse was about two weeks old, and by the time Jesse was six months old, we had no contact with his biological father.

I later discovered that Tony's violence in life had only escalated to unimaginable criminal levels. I gave him my heart, my body, my self-respect, and my security. I traded it all and for what? To be *told* I was loved; not *shown.*

I shared with no one what was going on. My family didn't like Tony, but that only made the relationship more satisfying to me.

I was out to prove a point, after all. I could not see that it would be at my own expense and the cost was much more than I could ever afford.

Looking at the house where so many other explosive scenes played out was so frustrating! The more I looked at that house, the more frustrated I got, but not with Tony. I was frustrated with myself.

'What were you thinking, Kim? How could you be so blind? How could you allow such awful things in the name of love? What a sick joke! You were so stupid!'

I noticed that I didn't aim any of this at my abuser. In fact, years earlier, I had forgiven him, but—obviously—I wasn't over it. There was still definitely someone I hadn't forgiven—myself. Even in this moment that was supposed to be for my healing, I just couldn't let myself off the hook.

I sat in my car replaying the memories and swimming in shame. In a dichotomy, I also thought about how far I had come since I was seventeen years old. Half of me was disgusted with and ashamed of myself. The other half was thankful to the Lord that I got myself and Jesse out when I did (and kind of proud of what I overcame).

I knew it was only by the grace of God that we both got out unharmed.

It wasn't easy. That boy didn't just let us go. He called. He showed up at my job and my house. He made death threats against us both. There were even times I would wake up in the middle of the night and he would be in my bedroom standing over me as I slept.

At seventeen years old, I went to the courthouse . . . by myself . . . to get a restraining order. I paid the county Sheriff to serve him with the papers. Most places don't make you pay anymore, but that's how it was done then. Pay for a restraining order that's worth about as much as the paper it's printed on. I'm still not sure where I found that strength, but I'm pretty sure it was in the innocent eyes of the new, little man in my life. Sometimes, your love for your child will make you do things that you would have never done just for yourself. I lived in fear that Tony would find us for many years. Even after getting married and moving away from my home town, nightmares of him standing over me as I slept shook me awake many times.

As I sat in front of that house of abuse, God's agenda ruled the day again and He revealed to me how deeply I still blamed myself. I recalled that the years of self-talk surrounding that relationship was completely shaming to myself. I could hear myself berating myself for being such a "sucker" over and over. I always wondered why it was so easy for me to forgive my abuser; now I could see that it was because I blamed myself!

God interrupted my thoughts with His and I began to see myself in that situation the way He did. I saw a fool, but He saw a broken, hurting little girl. I saw a failure, but He saw someone desperate enough to believe the enemy's lies. I saw someone who had no worth, but He saw someone worthy of His Love. At sixteen years old, I was a mother, but My Father only saw me as His child. I saw her with condemnation, but He saw Her with mercy.

God's Grace washed over me like a cleansing stream as I saw myself through His eyes of love. His love overwhelmed me, but old habits die hard and I can be a very slow learner. I still wasn't convinced. I respectfully reminded him that, before He poured out any more mercy on this fool, He should consider my last appeal to withhold His Grace from me:

With the way I was living back then, wasn't I just getting what I deserved?

I waited for His response.

"Not only did I my love rescue you from your pit, but I blessed you in the midst of it! Children are a gift of the Lord. The fruit of the womb is a reward from Me."

—Psalm 127

I was blown away by this revelation. When I deserved it the least, He blessed me the most! He gave me the gift of a child, a new life. Don't even get me started on how I processed the part about it being a reward! Why would He reward me when I was in rebellion toward Him and my parents?

Before I could even get the question out, He spoke:

"That's why it's called Grace."

His healing oil flowed over my soul, which was still quite tender from the beating I had just given it.

Grace. That's why it's called Grace.

He reminded me how I had insisted that, if I were going to have a son, his name would be Jesse. I knew that was my baby's name and I would not consider another. My mom even tried to talk me out of it, to no avail. It wasn't until Jesse was one year old that I learned what his name means:

A gift of God's Grace

My son's very life was a love note to me, a sinner, to be opened at the right moment, as evidenced by his name! I could hardly wrap my mind around a God so good that, when you are at your absolute worst, He gives you a gift. The gift of my son Jesse is exactly what I needed to wake me up from my anger-induced coma and to choose life once again.

To this day, I tell Jesse that he began fulfilling his destiny at conception. Not many people can say that, but he can. He is anointed to bring lives out of the darkness and into the glorious light. He began doing it while in the womb and mine was the first!

While I was pregnant, I spent many nights thinking

about what kind of mother I wanted to be. I remembered growing up to Bible stories read by my precious mom. I knew the Word because of those stories. I knew God was real because of those stories. Would I do the same for my son? As a teen, my life was the opposite of a mother reading Bible stories. Go ahead and use your imagination, you won't be far off.

I knew I couldn't read Bible Stories to him and then go off and party. That would be so hypocritical! I literally had to choose between Bible stories and partying! I knew if I kept living the way I was, my son would be robbed of the Truth.

That scared me, so I cried out, "Help me, God!" In fact, that became my constant prayer.

And He did.

Even the thoughts of the life I almost chose for my son made me feel ashamed and angry as I thought them. I heard the voice of the Lord urge me to forgive myself; to let myself off the hook. I knew that if my Creator could forgive me and I could not, I was somehow trying to overrule Him; and the last time I checked, I didn't have that kind of jurisdiction!

Forgiving myself became an act of obedience, not a feeling or even a strong desire. I don't know why I desired to hold this against myself, but it was time to let it go. I surrendered to His will. I repented (changed my mind to match His) and forgave myself. I accepted His forgiveness and released all my shame and anger into His hands. I finally accepted the grace and mercy He had for me all these years.

FREE!

I felt as though I was feeling His sense of relief! He was more relieved than I was? Yes, He was. He had been waiting for me to realize I was forgiven and to let it go. He knew that this was the source of my self-sabotaging bondage long before I did. Yet, He was so patient with me, waiting twenty-five years for me to be ready for this healing. I love that about Him!

The picture was clear now. I wasn't just looking at a house that held bad memories anymore. I was looking at the place that represented the moment that my sin and shame collided with GRACE!

Now, that is a grave I can dance on!

The Third Grave

The Place Where You Were Betrayed

*"Even my close friend, someone I trusted,
one who shared my bread, has turned
against me."*

— KING DAVID

*"There's a phrase, 'the elephant in the
living room,' which purports to describe
what it's like to live with a drug addict,
an alcoholic, an abuser. People outside
such relationships will sometimes ask,
'How could you let such a business go on
for so many years? Didn't you see the
elephant in the room?' And it's so hard
for anyone living in a more normal
situation to understand the answer that
comes closest to the truth; 'I'm sorry, but
it was there when I moved in.*

> *I didn't know it was an elephant; I*
> *thought it was part of the furniture.'*
> *There comes an aha-moment for some*
> *folks – the lucky ones – when they*
> *suddenly recognize the difference."*

—STEPHEN KING

*I*t was like I had come to a drive-in movie that day. On the big screen of my mind I saw the scene play out in completion. It was a fall day, in October, 1989, and I was lying in bed, next to my brand-new husband.

I met Doug in May of that same year, a few weeks before my high school graduation. We met at a young adult's Bible study at a local church that I began attending after Jesse was born. We fell for each other fast and hard.

I believed he was "the one" because I met him at church, at a Bible study, no less! He was the only guy I ever dated who even professed to have faith. I knew he was a Christian and that I was attracted to him. He made me feel wanted and special. He took a special interest in my son, who was approaching his first birthday and was lacking for a father. In fact, Jesse was more or less the reason we met. I was dropping Jesse off at the church nursery before the service when our eyes first locked. Who wouldn't fall for a young, cute guy who volunteered to work in the church nursery?

Up until that point, I dated a couple of other guys as a single teen mom but was very guarded. Well, all of that went right out the window with this Godsend that I met at church. What could possibly be wrong? I threw myself into this new relationship. He was different from the others because he had sincere faith, he helped me, and—most importantly—he cared for my son.

Although Doug and I met at a Bible study and were both trying to live better lives, I was soon pregnant again. We talked about getting married early in our relationship, before I even knew I was pregnant, so when the pregnancy test was positive, we decided to go ahead and do it. You may think that doesn't sound very romantic. It wasn't.

We rushed right into everything. Love, life, parenting, everything. (I now recognize that this was a red flag!) On October 13, 1989, we were married, five months after we met.

As I was heading to this drive-in of my past, I wondered, *'Why this particular house? We lived in five different homes while we were married. Why this one?'*

I would soon understand that God chose this house in Milwaukee, Wisconsin, to become the resting place of my eighteen-year marriage, because it was the place where the tumult began.

This was the third grave;
the place where I was betrayed.

The movie in my mind played on. As Doug and I lay there, in the dark, one week after we said, "I do," he said he had something to tell me.

It sounded ominous. I was worried about what he was going to say. I admit, something didn't seem right when we were dating. There were red flags, but nothing "solid" so I ignored them in hopes that they would not come back to haunt me later. If we just got married, everything would be okay.

My second child . . . our child . . . was due in March of 1990, and I believed that God had answered my prayers. My son finally had father, and I had the complete family I had always wanted! What I didn't know was that my trust would be betrayed. And not only once, but over and over again. The first time would be that night in bed when I heard those words—

"Kim, there's something I need to tell you."

"Okay, what is it?" I asked, matching his apprehensive tone.

After a long pause, he just said it.

"I'm addicted to drugs and drinking and I stole some of our wedding money and used it to buy cocaine. I just had to tell you."

I WAS STUNNED. I WAS SICKENED. I FELT TRICKED, TRAPPED, LIED TO.

I was stunned. I was sickened. I felt tricked, trapped, lied to. This was a hard truth I had never even considered, and it would be my reality for what I believed

-50-

at the time would be forever. That is exactly why the Lord chose to answer my question of "Why this place?" with this scene – this house. It was the birthplace of eighteen years of tricks, lies, and betrayal. That night was one of the rare moments he did tell me the whole truth and it was the beginning of a roller coaster ride that, up until that point, I had no idea even existed. Ironically, I also had something to tell him on that fateful evening.

"What is your secret?" he asked.

I hesitated for a moment and then told him, "I'm bulimic."

"What's that?" he asked.

"It is when you eat a lot of food and then throw it up afterwards."

He was perplexed as he asked, "Why?"

"I don't know, you just do."

"Well, stop it!" was his solution.

"It's not that easy." I stated.

What a marriage in the making we had! Two addicts, barely aware of how deep we were in our own pits, now with monogrammed shovels, digging one together.

This was definitely the hardest grave to reflect on. Not because I was still the walking wounded that I had been for so many years and it was too painful to recount. It was because this one house, this one grave, represented the majority of my adult life, from barely a young woman of eighteen years old to the age of thirty-six.

Eighteen years I spent on the threshing floor, beaten so that the wheat could be separated from the chaff, the good from the bad, in my heart. Even better stated, the useful was separated from the useless through storm after storm and test upon test. The circumstances were just the precursor to the real storm . . . the one that raged inside me. So many of my storms were self-inflicted. This grave represented the death place of so many monsters that lurked inside me! Here, his ugliness brought out my ugliness until it was all destroyed and just a pile of ashes. But my Lord promises to make beauty from ashes (Isaiah 61:3) and, I assure you, those ashes have been transformed into the beauty I now behold.

Do you know anyone who grew up with alcoholism or chemical addiction? Maybe it was you or maybe you are married to an alcoholic or the child of an addict. If so, then you probably know exactly what I mean by ugliness and ashes. If you are reading this and aren't making the connection, it is my hope that you will only know of the realities of addiction from what you read or see on TV.

The list of uglies that comes with alcoholism seems never-ending, but it is not my intent to point out anyone else's list here. In order for this roller coaster ride to consume my life for eighteen years, I had to participate to some degree. After all, I was on the ride and no one put a gun to my head to make me stay there against my will. So, it is here that I chose to identify my part in that movie where the same scene was featured year after year and I faithfully read my lines as the enabler.

As my brilliant therapist once put it, alcoholism is only 5% alcohol and the other 95% is the "ism." The ism is the ugliest of the ugly part. It is all of the dysfunction that the actors in this tragic film learn to rely upon and accept as normal life. The ism is all of the poor coping and relationship skills that break down and corrode relationships faster than any liquid or chemical ever could. And the ism is in all of the roles of the film, not just the addict. Baggage attracts baggage, and the addict relies heavily on this fact. Not sure about this? Ask yourself if you see any ism in you.

It looks like any or all of these: denial, enabling, manipulating, controlling, blame-shifting, switching, finger-pointing, refusal to take responsibility, taking too much responsibility, fear, anger, covering up, lying, cheating, stealing, rescuing, and too many more to list.

For years, I believed that if Doug would just stay sober, we'd be home free. Little did I know, that sobriety would've only put us 5% ahead. We still had the 95% ism to go. That 95% isn't in a bottle that you can dump out. It's in your heart.

I sat at this gravesite and my first response was gratitude! (Clearly, I was starting to trust this whole joy and dancing thing, because I know how ridiculous that sounds.) When I had the revelation of the betrayal and how it played out over and over, always the same principal, but different details, I found myself . . . smiling.

Sound crazy? Maybe. But I had good reason! I thought about the "woman" I was lying in that bed that night—a night that seemed like a hundred years ago—and I rejoiced.

I am not her anymore!

Thank you, Lord!

The wounds of betrayal where love and trust were supposed to thrive is exactly what God used to change me.

I pledged my heart to serve Jesus shortly after my twenty-first birthday. He became my Savior when I was little, but my Lord?

Not so much.

From my teen years until the third year of my marriage, I did what I wanted and thought best—and I had all of the emptiness to prove it. By then, The Lord had already delivered me from my own teenaged alcohol and drug problem. (I still tell my kids, but for the Grace of God, they could have easily grown up with two alcoholic parents.) God saved me from death and destruction in many forms during my first twenty-one years . . . in spite of myself.

Yes, saving He did well and I knew Him as Savior, but I certainly hadn't made him *Lord* over my marriage or my eating disorder. I wasn't interested in making him the Lord of my life. That is, until I was on the roller coaster of my marriage for a while. I became pretty desperate for a better life, a better way. It was time to graduate from crying out for help all the time. It was time to learn to obey Him. I wanted more than a 911 line to God. I wanted peace. I wanted the friend I could call on anytime just to chat, not only in crisis times. I had a simple conversation with God that changed my life dramatically.

"Lord, I know about you, but I know I am not living for you. I don't even really know what that means, but please show me how to do it."

I then declared my decision publicly by being baptized just before my twenty-first birthday. It was a new beginning and I had new hope. I was excited to begin my new life with God!

Part of my new life of surrender was a decision to totally trust God to plan our family.

To trust God with my womb was a nerve-wracking choice and I did not make it rashly or lightly! I already had three children by the age of twenty-one. My nickname was Fertile Myrtle. I was sure that this decision was the equivalent of moving into a shoe and having so many kids that I wouldn't know what to do. Yet I couldn't deny a sense of destiny wrapped up in all of the thoughts and feelings I had surrounding this decision. I felt called to trust God with my womb. I felt called to be His vessel to bring forth lives He marked with destiny! I wanted so much to trust Him with every single area of my life.

I was willing, but afraid, so I sought God in the only way I knew how to, which was to wait for some kind of answer or sign that I was on the right track. Not surprisingly, He delivered. To quell my fears about financially providing for my children, He assured me that if I sought first His kingdom and His righteousness, He would add all other things. (Matthew 6:33.) We were young, not college educated, and already had three children. When praying about my fear of providing for such a brood with a good friend, the Lord gave her a vision. She saw a mama bird feeding all of her baby birds with one big fat worm. Peace flooded my heart as I knew My Provider would not fail me. However, in my humanness, I just had to know how many baby birds she saw.

She said, "Six."

I was relieved. "Six. Okay. Six. I think I can handle six. Okay."

Which is exactly why He only put six in the vision! He knew I was silly enough to believe that I could handle six and that it wouldn't scare me into a convent.

Allow me to go on record confessing that I was a fool to believe I could handle any, let alone six. In hindsight, I can say I wasn't even handling the three I already had very well! Thank God He didn't put eleven birds in that nest. I think I would've headed for the hills. Yes, I gave birth to eleven beautiful, miraculous children. Each one represents the Heritage that I have been generously given by the same God who changed Abram's name to Abraham which means "father of a multitude." I am, for all intents and purposes, the mother of a multitude. Just come over at Christmastime and you will be a believer.

Whether I was destined to have six or sixteen children, I knew in the deepest part of me that this was my calling. After prayer and many discussions with my husband over the course of a month, we said, "Yes," to God.

I would trust God as I ministered to my children the same way missionaries do in Zimbabwe. My mission field would begin with my womb. I would offer all to Jesus and allow Him to make a miracle out of my life and my family. *Little did I know how desperately we would need one.* I was afraid we would not be able to meet the needs of a large family, but I would have to trust Him to provide as I knew all too well what our limitations were.

FREE!

And did He deliver! I could fill a book with stories of His miraculous provision. Over the years, countless needs were met through prayer and God's faithfulness. Things like food, socks, shoes, even bras that miraculously fit, cars,

> I COULD FILL A BOOK WITH STORIES OF HIS MIRACULOUS PROVISION.

money for bills, homes, friendships, brooms, furniture, trips, baby items, school books and supplies. A fifteen-passenger van even showed up in my driveway on my daughter Ella's third birthday. We celebrated "her" birthday present!

When He says to seek Him first and not worry about what you will eat, drink, or wear, He means it! The decision to trust God to plan my family and provide for us was one of the best decisions I ever made.

About two months after giving my womb to God, I learned I was pregnant with my fourth child. Eventually, I would give birth to a total of six sons and five daughters. Each child arrived with a destiny and purpose of their own! Together, the Lord told me, we would see them raised up for His glory. Many times, my imagination would run with the possibilities. Maybe I was holding a future president, or missionary, or the doctor who would cure cancer.

'Was I holding the next Billy Graham? After all, he only had one mother.'

Whatever the future held, it excited and thrilled me while simultaneously putting me on my knees in prayer.

I cried out to God to help me prepare these Sons and Daughters of Destiny to be every bit of who He created them to be. Motherhood was my ministry and it would prove to stretch me.

In the meantime, Doug's addiction grew worse. I became an A-class enabler, too. My church leadership taught me that if I was a submissive, godly wife, then my husband would see the light, so to speak, and God would transform our mess into a marriage. So, for a season, I mostly kept my mouth shut about Doug's behavior, except for the occasional blowup.

He used drugs and alcohol regularly, lied frequently, reneged on most commitments he made to me and the kids, missed a lot of work, and expected me to cover up and lie for him. I bailed us out of a lot of situations and, slowly, grew resentful.

I tried to be the best mother and wife that I could be. What I did not know then is that, when you allow manipulation, blame shifting, and deception without confronting it, not only will there be no change in the other person, but you will end up feeling wildly resentful and powerless. I know this because that is exactly what happened to me. I believed that I had no other choices in my situation. I became fearful, angry, and resentful. Better stated, I chose to become fearful and angry in response to my incredibly overwhelming sense of powerlessness.

I wish not to recount the years I spent angry, miserable, and lashing out at everyone around me. All that was ugly in me was revealed. I have asked my children to forgive me for how my poor coping skills, fear, anger, and frustration with my life affected them. They deserved so much love and affirmation and I was an emotional train wreck much of the time, so they did not get it. No matter how difficult or unmanageable my emotions were, my deepest desire was to please God, to be a good wife, and be a loving mother. Those desires are what kept me seeking God with all my heart and not giving up.

Eventually, I took every ounce of my ugly to God. I brought a broken heart, a bitter root, and a skewed definition of love. The pain of not being loved the way I needed to be was too much for me to handle on my own. I decided to start trusting God for deliverance from the struggles in my life.

Most of my deliverances throughout my walk with God have been processes, not hallelujah moments or instant miracles. However, bulimia was one time when God just touched me, and it left me. The way it happened was, at age twenty-one, when I began to walk with the Lord and get in his word, I discovered the John 8:36 that says, "So if the Son sets you free, you will be free indeed."

I was desperate to get free of the cycle of binging and purging. I would say "God, you said I'm free and I'm not. You're not a Liar. Can you make this true for me, please? Can you make this word not seem like a contradiction in my life?"

I prayed that for years. I remember one day waking up and thinking "something's different." The desire for the old relationship with food was just . . . gone. I was free. For several years I had prayed; then, I just stopped at twenty-six.

With constant proofs of God's faithfulness and goodness, I trusted Him with even bigger challenges. I longed for my husband to love me as passionately as he did drugs and alcohol.

I would cry out, "Lord, when am I going to be free to love and to be loved?"

I felt like I had lived in a loveless prison under the guise of love my whole life. This marriage wasn't any different from all of the other relationships in my life. My dream for myself was shattered and now I was now raising my children in that same prison! That was the thing I dreaded the most.

God heard my cries and began to set me free one chain link at a time.

First, He told me to love my husband the way I wanted to be loved. My reaction was less than enthusiastic. What? I have to give love without receiving any? This thought left me feeling empty inside and a little irritated, to be honest. Why do I always have to be the one to take the high road? I fought it for a while and then the gentle persistent nudging of the Holy Spirit prevailed. My repentance and my willingness opened up the way in my heart to begin to offer love and see others the way God sees them. It wasn't easy, but it felt great! God knew I needed to first receive His love and then give it in order to receive revelation of what it really is and what it isn't.

I began to see that some of the things (okay; a lot of the things) I did in the name of love . . . *were not out of love at all.*

Somewhere in my mind echoed the verse, "Perfect love casts out all fear." (1 John 4:18) So, it must follow that, if I were to love with God's love, then I wouldn't do things out of fear. Talk about a light bulb moment! Fear was my motivator, not love!

All my years of covering up for my husband's addiction, dishonesty and disrespect, and protecting him (or so I thought) were because I feared what would happen to me and the kids if I stood up. I had not even considered what was best for him, either. I was afraid of being rejected and alone. I was doing what would make him comfortable because, if he was comfortable, then I didn't have to worry about him rejecting or abandoning me.

My love was a counterfeit version born out of selfishness, but given under the guise of love. I now know first-hand that love does what is best for the other person, not what feels best for that person...no matter what the cost. Love does not seek its own. (1 Corinthians 13).

My selfish brand of love for my husband put me in the pit alongside him, with a shovel in my hand, and it was time to climb out. How else could I throw him a rope?

First, I took total responsibility for my part in the mess. I owned it and actively worked on it. I hated feeling so disrespected by him and by the kids, but I had never taken responsibility for the disrespect I doled out.

I discovered new ways to handle volatile situations without crossing the line from respect into disrespect. I worked so hard on my own mouth and my own temper. It seemed like such a long, slow process, but it was only then that I could begin to love my husband and my children better. I called it loving them higher. Everything changed, especially me. I changed how I handled my husband's addiction. I didn't cover anything up or look in the other direction. I didn't bail him out or take on all of the responsibility and only allow him to take a little. I respectfully set and enforced boundaries – something I did not know how to do for most of my life.

As much as I knew that this was the right thing to do, I was still afraid of what would happen to me. Would he reject me? Would he punish me? Would he abandon me? Would I end up alone, again? I did it anyway, in the face of my fears. I confronted the addiction and every ugly thing that came with it . . . first in me, then in him.

Fear had been my constant companion, but now I had a new companion that I did not recognize. It was peace – the kind of peace only obedience to God can provide. I felt safer than ever, because I knew the promises of God for His children who trust and obey. I finally felt like I was one of those children. I had the assurance only God can give when we are tracking with Him. It was a really good feeling. Heaven was behind me, and all of us. I believed more than ever that this family had a shot at restoration.

Ultimately, I learned and accepted that I could only make decisions for me. Oh, how I wished I could make decisions for us all, and God knows I tried, but it was up to each of us to choose our own path. Would my husband align himself with the Will of the Father, get honest about his addiction, and work to overcome it, or not? Only time would tell.

I got to face my fears of rejection and abandonment head-on when they came true. Doug was not happy with this epiphany I had or the way I was living it out. He became very angry with me, punished me with more rejection, and I was definitely alone. By then, I realized how silly it was for me to even fear being alone! It was no different from how I had been living anyway! I had already been alone. When you love someone with an addiction, you live a life of isolation. I was alone at events, alone in my bed at night, alone at church many times, alone with the children. And I was alone for all the wrong reasons, so I reasoned that I might as well feel alone for the right ones! I boldly said, 'No,' where I normally said yes.

No, I will not bail us out of this jam.

No, I will not lie for you.

No, I will not keep this incident a secret.

Instead, I will talk to our pastor.

I will call the police.

I will speak to your probation officer if you use drugs in our home.

I love you too much to help you destroy your life.

I love you too much to help you destroy this family.

I love myself too much to help you destroy me.

As the light grew brighter for me and others around us, I could see things for what they really were and how they had affected my children. A lot of things came to the surface and I slowly learned that an incredible amount of damage had been done. More than I thought. I also began to see that their parents' skewed version of love had rubbed off on my children.

"Isn't love helping no matter what?" they asked me. "Isn't loyalty never saying no?"

"No."

In fact, those things are manipulation. They are the essence of the ism. They are corrosive and deadly to healthy, happy marriages and families and allowing them in my home was not honoring anyone, least of all my husband.

Some questions, posed to me by an older, wiser believer, slapped me into reality:

Does it honor someone when when you allow them to manipulate and lie to you?
Does it honor someone when you stoop to their level, maniputlating or lying in return?

Does it honor someone when you allow them to renege on promises to protect and provide for loved ones?

That is not honor.

Honor rejoices in righteousness.

Honor says, "You can do better and so can I."

Honor says, "I love you too much to allow your manipulation to work on me."

Bestselling speaker, author, and Christian teacher, Joyce Meyer, teaches that you can't spend years creating a mess and then expect to clean it up in one day. Well, we had worked long and hard to make our mess, so it wasn't going away any time soon. It was a slow process, so I learned to practice patience. By practice, I mean the kind of practicing that happens when your child comes home from fourth grade music class with his first recorder. The whole family has to wear ear plugs while they're "practicing." I practiced patience like that. I was never good at patience. I'm impetuous and anxious by nature, but the Lord always gave me what I needed for each day, one day at a time.

With the support of others, I was ready to really confront the addiction and Doug's need for treatment. I was finally ready to do it with love and respect. I could finally say 'Enough!' for the right reasons, with the right heart: not because it was inconvenient for me to be married to an addict, but because he was killing himself slowly and I may be the only one who could stop him from succeeding.

What a victory for this selfish, fearful heart!

God gave me eyes to see my husband and children the way He does: as whole, healed, victorious warriors in His Kingdom.

I spoke it over them, into them, and around them. Nothing is impossible with God! I saw my husband as a prisoner of the enemy's lies and prayed for God to break him out! My heart began to expand to hold the love that I longed for all my life.

Yet, it in other ways, this was the most painful time I have ever known. The anger and hostility I received from the ones I loved cut me to the core. I've since learned that when God decides to cut something into your heart, He must first cut something else out. He cut out of me the desire to please and be affirmed by man and cut into me an insatiable hunger to live and breathe for an audience of One. I could love like this, not to be loved in return, but to please my God.

I wanted my love to fling a door open for my husband and children to go higher, like God's love did for me. I longed for us all to get better . . . but I could only do my part. I would give this love, even if they did not take it.

Spurred on by real love and his escalating behavior, I took drastic measures. I called on a man who was twenty years sober, who loved the Lord, and who was a source of support to both of us. I told him I planned to confront Doug and asked this man to be present. He said yes.

When the night came, I was calm. I was prayed up

and full of love and hope when I said, "Enough is enough. This has to stop. We are all in danger. It's like we have built a coffee table bit by bit over the years. We keep adding to it while the kids are playing on it. They are setting their drinks on in it, putting their feet up on it, and playing with their toys on it, but—the thing of it is—this coffee table is made of dynamite! I know its dynamite; you know its dynamite; but we just keep pretending it's just a coffee table. It isn't a coffee table; it is a bomb and I will not help build it anymore. It needs to be disassembled and removed for everyone's sake or this whole place and everyone in it is going up in flames. This addiction has got to go! It has got to go, or . . . me and the kids? We have got to go."

I told him that I loved him too much to keep helping him kill himself. His health was seriously deteriorating and we were only in our mid-thirties. Our family doctor, who had a very mild bedside manner, told him very aggressively that his heart was a ticking time bomb. There was more at stake than ever. It was time for me to take action.

To prove my words had meaning, I confronted him with our friend present as a witness and gave him the summer to complete the list of steps he needed to take toward recovery. I continued getting help for myself and working on my own coping skills while I watched and waited. I told him that if he did not comply by summer's end, the kids and I would move out.

Sadly, he did not get the help he needed. Things grew worse. One day in August, while he was at work, the kids and I moved out of the house. We packed up only what we needed, had friends come with trucks and trailers, and we were out in one day.

We moved into the home of dear friends. Eventually, Doug did seek treatment and, after seven months and much marriage counselling, we reconciled. Six months after we reconciled, he had a total relapse and, from there, things, shot downward faster than ever.

Those were the last days of our marriage.

Ultimately, Doug decided he was "....not interested in this new brand of love."

He told me that word-for-word. I was okay hearing it, though, because it wasn't my love or my idea. It was God's way of loving and His Love gets rejected every day, by most of the world! I was in good company, I reasoned. I'd rather model God's kind of love and healthy boundaries to my children, anyway. They had lived on the "Jerry Springer Show" for long enough.

Ultimately, the more I enforced healthy boundaries and the stronger I became, the bigger the messes he created. He spiralled completely out of control into more drinking, more drugs, more lies, more trouble with the law, more relationships destroyed, and less of a marriage to sober up for. I was a prisoner again, but this time, one of a different sort.

I was "a prisoner of hope," as it says in Zechariah 9:12. God promised to deliver us so many times, I lost count. I truly trusted him with the uncertain future! I cried out to God for the strength and wisdom to keep living and loving this new way, so that my children may see and know the love of God.

By 2007, Doug was in and out of legal custody and treatment programs too many times to count. He spent the first eight months of that year in jail, a half-way house, or in court ordered treatment. A month after our eighteenth wedding anniversary, when he learned that I was contemplating divorce, he snapped.

On November 14, 2007, he began drinking hard and fast, earlier than usual. I left home at five o'clock to work my part time job at a department store. He was home with the kids, who told me later that they were scared, because he was very angry and hostile. At around nine o'clock he got into his van and drove to my workplace. He planned to take his anger out on me, but I was "safe" in a public place. He did manage to harass, threaten, and intimidate me (not to mention embarrass me). He attracted the attention of strangers, as well as the store managers – enough to have the police called on him. When asked to leave, repeatedly by my manager, he finally did, but not until he flattened a tire on my van, leaving me stranded at a closed department store at ten-thirty at night. I called my children to let them know their dad was on a rampage . . . not a pleasant call to make, by the way.

Doug drove straight home and was filled with such fury that, combined with my phone call, my children knew to hide.

My seventeen-year-old daughter, Taylor, hid in her bedroom. Doug broke down the bedroom door of her room and lunged at her on the bed.

While she forced herself as far away from her as she could, against the wall, he tried to pull her down where he could strike her. He struck Taylor with his fist while she screamed in terror and tried to break his hold on her. My son, Alex, who was only fifteen himself, valiantly jumped in between them and restrained his father as my Taylor daughter dialled 911 with her phone behind her back. Alex tackled his dad to the ground and had to hold him there until the police came.

I finally arrived home, not sure what to expect. Taylor and Alex were at the kitchen table filling out police reports and I had to join in, not just to input what I knew of this incident, but of Doug's actions earlier in the night.

With two of his children bruised and battered, eight more who were scarred by what they heard and saw, and me in shock at all of it, Doug was arrested and removed from our home.

Forever.

In one fateful and very dark moment, it was over. All of it. Eighteen years of ugly ended in one of the most hideous displays you could imagine. He was forcibly removed by the police and taken into custody . . . never to return to our home or our family.

All of those years that I believed in God's promise of newness for my family, I never once imagined the end would come on the heels of such a violent event.

Before you go thinking that God failed me, please listen closely: *God did not intend for that violent end.* God intended for my husband to repent and walk in the light. That was and still is His will. But God gives people the ability to choose for themselves which way they will live and who or what they will serve. He allows us to reap the consequences of those choices, too, whether good or bad.

In our case, Doug's bad choices and the consequences thereof affected a lot of innocent lives, each of our eleven children. The reality of this injustice can be hard to swallow. That is precisely why Jesus went to The Cross—to provide the solution, the medicine, and the antidote for every kind of injustice that touches the human race. God's Love and Power are enough to heal all of us; from everything.

It is up to each of us whether we align our will with His and His healing becomes our healing. I do not blame

> IT IS UP TO EACH OF US WHETHER WE ALIGN OUR WILL WITH HIS.

the God I trusted for what happened to my children; I trust the God I know and love to heal my children of the wounds they incurred from fallen and deeply flawed parents.

After that fateful night, we were all shell-shocked for some time, but relieved. My children had never felt so unsafe and afraid and I made the decision never to ask them to live that way again. The criminal court implemented a "No Contact Order" and, for the first time in years, I felt safe. I filed a domestic abuse restraining order that same day. I didn't have to pay for it that time.

In the courthouse, I sat with a female advocate assigned to assist me with the restraining order. She handed me a sheet of paper, one of many, and asked me to fill this one out first. It was a list of things that are considered abusive. She asked me to circle all that applied. When I was finished, I counted only two things that I did not circle. I had experienced every other thing but two on that sheet of paper in my eighteen years of marriage. That meant my kids did, too. It was a wake-up call I needed and hated all at once. I began to cry.

As I looked at a standardized form, checking off all of the ways we had been abused, threatened, neglected, or wrongfully confronted over the years (yeah . . . just the fact that they make standard forms for that stuff was tough), I realized, in black and white, the life to which my children had been exposed.

"I know this is very painful for you," she offered.

"Oh, I am not crying for me," I assured her.

"Then why are you crying?"

"I am crying for my children."

I held up the ominous paper full of circles. The paper that was evidence I had spent the last eighteen years as abused as I had been on the landing of my staircase while expecting my first baby at age sixteen.

With a shaky but firm tone I told her, "For years, I taught my kids that THIS is what love is. Mark my words. Never again!"

"I believe you," she said. "I really do."

I filed for a divorce two weeks later when the Lord miraculously provided the funds for an attorney.

So, what of the love that I gave and was not returned? Was it wasted? I wondered.

"The love you have given will be returned to you in abundance. For it is written: Do not be deceived, God is not mocked; for whatever a man sows, that will he also reap." (Galatians 6:7) The Lord assured me.

He told me that His law of reaping and sowing even applies to seeds of love, and that I would not be disappointed. I should have known that already, as one of the promises I clung to was Isaiah 49:23 which says:

Then you will know that I am the Lord; those who hope in me will not be disappointed.

As far as deliverance goes, He delivered! Not the way I thought He would, of course, but He delivered. He promised to make all things new. He has. He promised to heal my children's hearts. He is. He promised to restore our brokenness. He is. He promised that I would still fulfil my destiny. I am. *He is faithful!*

The difference between that eighteen-year-old-barely-a-woman who lay in that bed a week after her wedding and the almost-forty-woman sitting in the car staring at grave number three is vast.

I am no longer a victim; I am a victor.
I am no longer bitter; I am better.

I walked through the fiery furnace and can testify that the "fourth man" was with me! And, like my brothers before me, I can say that the only thing burned were the ropes that bound me. He used my fiery furnace to speed up the process that set me free to be loved by Him and to love in return. It was in this marriage that I received a Love that neither my husband or this world could offer me, but God did. And I was hooked.

With that love, God gave me other incredible breakthroughs and deliverances that, after the end, I was able to see with new eyes.

I moved from bitterness - forgiveness for the people whose actions hurt me, whether intentional or unintentional. I released them, and myself in turn.

I moved from anger to self-control. God saved me from me. I was always my biggest obstacle. He used my first husband's garbage to reveal my own.

I moved from entitlement to gratitude, fully appreciative of the gifts in my life.

I moved from self-pity to empowerment for using the tools and skills God gave me for my life.

Out of that eighteen-year journey, I discovered a genuine belief that my life could be everything God said it could be.

Recounting this part of my Wilderness alone with My Redeemer, I began to honor and worship Him for knowing exactly which threshing floor was most suitable for me. I thanked my Potter for this particular wheel and every sharp instrument used to create the vessel I was becoming. I thanked Him for patiently leading me through that wilderness where there were so many dry and weary days.

Like the sojourners of old, my wilderness was covered in a cloud of protection by day and a pillar of fire for warmth by night. Water flowed from rocks and Heaven gave its bread to feed me. I shudder to think of who I might be today if the Lord had left me how I was. I still trust Him completely to finish what He started in me all those years ago.

I cried tears of joy and gratitude. Knowing this story is not over, I rejoiced in what is still to come! My heart is so full of expectancy knowing there are many more testimonies of His Power and Love yet to be told from that wandering place!

Many more stories in my life and in my children's lives have been promised.

Though a rugged and dangerous climb, I stand with many treasures I picked up along the way: I know who I am in Christ. I am no longer a slave to the fear of man. I am no longer an enabler. I am an "EMPOWERER." My heart is free to love and to be loved. Finally! My long quest for love is over! This place of betrayal represented the greatest source of love I will ever know—God's love, shed abroad in my heart! It was worth every tear, every prayer and every minute I spent waiting for it. Not only do I rejoice over it, but if I had it to do all over again, I wouldn't change a thing.

God once told me, when I was complaining about my husband and marriage to Him, that I would be more thankful for Doug than anyone else in my life. I laughed out loud. Now, here I sat, in my car, thanking God for him, for the mess, for all of it. No, I would not want to remove this betrayal, this struggle, or this pain from my story. Why tamper with perfection? God's way is tailored, for you, for me, and it's brilliant. This grave was always meant to be a death that brought forth so much life in more ways than one. Now it is the perfect dance floor for this girl.

FREE!

The Fourth Grave

The Place Where You Were Orphaned

*Father of orphans, champion of widows,
is God in his holy house.*

—PSALM 68:6 MSG

*I will not leave you as orphans
[comfortless, desolate, bereaved, forlorn,
helpless]; I will come [back] to you.*

—JOHN 14:18 AMP

*I*t was so dark out, I was concerned that I wasn't going to be able to find this grave. I struggled to remember where it was. I hadn't been here in a long, long time and I had never been here after dark before. Most people don't visit actual graves at night, but tonight I wasn't like most people. To complicate matters further, this cemetery was huge and not at all well-lit. I drove in the way I remembered, but still found myself in unfamiliar territory. So I drove back out and then entered once again, trying a different path. I thought I'd found it! My headlights were the only source of light in this section of the cemetery and the headstone was laid in the ground, so I was not able to see what I was looking for from inside of the car. I maneuvered the car, parking it so my high beams were aimed in what I thought was the right direction. I grabbed my cell phone to use as a flashlight as I got out of the car.

I have to admit, it was creepy! I was definitely re-thinking my idea of coming here at night, but a single working mom with eight kids at home (three had left the nest) doesn't have much flexibility in her schedule. In addition, I only had three days left until the Feast of Tabernacles was to end and I knew what my marching orders were. So, I marched on . . . with The Lord . . . in a dark cemetery. God's a funny guy sometimes, isn't He?

I wandered around pointing my cell phone at every grave I passed.

'Where are you, Mom?'

Well, that's a ridiculous question, I thought. She's not here! I knew exactly where she was. She was (and is) in Heaven, and she had been since June 30, 1994.

I was a couple weeks shy of my twenty-third birthday when I lost my mom to cancer. She battled for almost two years before the tumor returned and she learned it was inoperable. She had herself a staredown with death, and she was going to win. Gracefully. And she did. She got her house in order, took care of all of her unfinished business in this life, and peacefully awaited her appointed time to meet her Savior. All of this while in constant pain. She couldn't speak because her voice box had been removed. She was slowly dying a painful death of malnutrition and dehydration because she could not swallow.

My mother had an amazing Spirit and I was privileged to be her daughter.

Never, during all those battles we had when I was a teenager, did I imagine, 'What if I only have five or six years left with her?'

No, most kids don't. The Lord knew and bringing reconciliation to my mom and me was the first thing He did for me when I made Him my Lord at the age of twenty-one. I am eternally grateful, because shortly after that is when she told us she had cancer.

I had watched my mom struggle for love for years and then watched her struggle for her life. My mom told us the story of when my dad asked her to marry him.

She said she prayed and asked God, "Should I marry him?"

The Lord replied with words I will never forget. "Marry him if you are willing to wait a very long time to be loved."

She decided to marry him anyway! I remember, after their divorce, wondering if my mom wished she had said no to my dad. I didn't have to wonder very long because she quickly reminded us that, if she hadn't married our dad, she wouldn't have us!

My mom said she had no regrets. I have since had the same conversation with my kids.

Much like my own, my mom's desire for love went unfulfilled. In fact, at the time of her death, the only love she ever really experienced was from God himself. She died at the tragically young age of forty-six after living a life full of pain. It was difficult to watch her suffer and I was so happy for her when her suffering ended. Many people have asked me how I could have peace with God when he took my mother at such a young age, especially after all of the prayers lifted on her behalf. The answer is easy. God gave me His peace with all of the events surrounding my mom's life and death.

A couple weeks after the funeral, I pondered this question for myself. I asked the Lord why He didn't heal her and give her the desires of her heart. This, of course, was what we all wanted for her.

His reply was, "Oh, I did! You should see her now!"

He told me how He Himself wanted to love her – and that even if He healed her and gave her every good thing on this earth, she would still experience pain, because there is tribulation in this world. He brought her to Himself, in every way, because of His love for her. Then He led me to James 1:12 which says:

"Blessed is the one who perseveres under trial because, having stood the test, that person will receive the crown of life that the Lord has promised to those who love him."

As I pictured a crown being placed on my precious mother's head, I remembered that, weeks before her death, she received a vision of herself wearing a crown. She believed that vision was intended to give her peace with dying. That vision wasn't just for her peace, it was for mine. I knew she passed her test and could now reap her eternal reward.

God was saying, *'She did it! She passed! She received her crown!'*

Why would I want her to stay here and suffer further? I was at complete peace. I marvelled at the love and faithfulness of God, and the Grace that He demonstrated in my mother's life. As much as I learned about the Lord through my mom's death, I learned even more through her life.

For a time, when I was young, and then again before her death, my mother personified faith. She spent hours in prayer. She loved the Lord and she loved to worship Him. She believed God would provide her big things – crazy things. And, mostly, she got them!

She once prayed for a friend's broken washing machine. It was a shared unit in her friend's apartment building. After my mom prayed, it worked—but only for her friend! No one else! She boldly shared her faith with others to the point of embarrassment for my younger self. She loved people with God's love, opening our home to single mothers and their children time and time again. She would give you the shirt off her back.

But she was broken and human and this life's pain took her out of the game for a long period of time. Some of her own wounds were too much for her to bear. Her trust was fragile and it took one too many hits. When that final blow hit her, when her divorce was final and God did not bring my father home, she stopped trusting everyone; including God. She struggled and suffered for years, but when she finally got back out on the field, her days were numbered by cancer. In true "Leta" fashion, she made the most of them! Even stricken with debilitating pain, she enjoyed her kids, her beloved grandchildren, and her life. She gave and asked nothing in return. She worshipped God with all of her heart, even with no vocal chords, a tracheotomy, and a fatal tumor in her throat. No matter how bad the pain or prognosis, she remained in her rediscovered faithfulness.

I will never forget the day I realized that the faithful, Jesus-loving mom I knew as a young child was back. I was sitting with her, talking about God. By this time, her voice box had been removed, so she would mouth her words, but no sound would come out. We all came to understand her fairly quickly. I was telling her that I was learning what rejoicing in the Lord meant. I told her that one of the meanings was to spin or twirl about wildly.

A tear left her eye and landed on her leg as she told me, "The Lord has been telling me to rejoice in Him, and that is exactly what I've been picturing myself doing as I worship Him."

I was speechless. Her body wouldn't allow her to rejoice physically, but nothing would stop her soul and spirit from obeying and rejoicing in her God.

I am so proud of my mom and pray that I am the strong, resilient woman that she was. Her courage and impact were further demonstrated at her funeral. Countless people came up to me and my sisters to say wonderful things about her and to tell us how my mom changed their lives.

"It was your mom that led me to the Lord."

"Thanks to your mom, I know Jesus!" On and on.

What surprised me so was that many of those people were people she met and befriended during her days spent not walking with the Lord. I was shocked to discover that she was still telling others about Jesus in the midst of her own faith crisis. God was faithful to water every seed that she had sown. In the end, I was even more amazed at what she accomplished in the midst of her life of suffering than during her glory days.

Life without my mother has not been easy or painless. I can honestly say I have peace with God about my mom's death, but there have been painful times along the way. Mother's Day has been particularly challenging. The first one after her death was excruciating. I cried all day long with this one realization: I don't have a mother. I couldn't wrap my mind around the fact that I would never be able to call someone, "Mom" again . . . to go home to Mom's . . . or to answer my phone and say, "Oh, hi Mom!"

It was too much to grasp. I ached so badly to hear her voice and feel her hug. I cried so hard and longed so much to feel like I had a parent to love me, that I called my dad. He did his best to comfort me, but he wasn't my mom.

While talking to my sister, Kelly, that same day, she told me that she had just learned the true definition of an orphan: It is a child who has lost their mother. Webster's 1828 Dictionary defines an orphan as: a child who is bereaved of his father or mother or both. By definition, I was an orphan.

All of these thoughts and emotions stirred in my mind like a bittersweet soup as I searched that dark night for my mother's grave. Then, the most frustrating thing happened – I couldn't find it!

I couldn't believe that I couldn't find my own mother's grave! I bounced back and forth between anger and guilt. *'What kind of daughter can't find her own mom's grave? What in the world is wrong with me?'*

Disheartened, I gave up on my search and made my way back to the car feeling totally defeated.

Once in the car, I felt the Lord settle my heart and say, "It's okay. We both know it's here."

**The fourth grave was an actual grave;
the place where I was orphaned.**

'But Lord, I thought that every stop would be perfect and I'd have my moment at each one! I mean, how do I dance on a grave that I can't even find?' (Not that I would have actually danced on my mother's grave. I'm strictly speaking figuratively!)

His peace prevailed and I felt Him nudge me. He was nudging me toward the good once again, reminding me I was here for the joy He promised me.

And there was joy! I remembered two incredible things that happened to me after my mom died.

The first was between God and me. I had heard about the Love of God, but had not really experienced it. Being orphaned left me so empty and broken. What I did not realize at the time was that it also opened up my heart to receive the Father's love like never before. The bigger the void I felt, the more I sought His Love, the more I sought His Love, the more of it He poured out on me. When He was all I had, I discovered that He was all I needed. His love became tangible to me. I became his daughter and not just in name. I discovered what was rightfully mine as a co-heir with Christ, and I began to access it!

One particular night, I sat at my kitchen table to read the Word and to journal. I encountered a verse about love. I sat there wishing I could experience it and not just read about it. I wanted to FEEL it. I reached out to Heaven and something supernatural happened . . . Heaven reached back! In an instant, I felt it. I felt loved by God!

FREE!

Words can hardly describe how it feels to have a tidal wave of God's Love pour into your soul and swirl around your insides making you warm. My emotions felt lifted in a way no human interaction can lift them. My mind; perplexed! How can this be, that the Creator of the Universe, the One I have sinned against so many times, feels like this about me? Oh, but I would not turn it down! I drank it in and revelled in it with joy and awe at the same time. I finally felt and understood how loved I was, how special I was, and how chosen I was. I no longer needed to believe this by faith, I knew it as my reality. And from His heart of love, the blessing began to flow in my life.

Because God is as much practical as He is spiritual, He did not stop there! The most wonderful thing happened after that. The Lord brought not one, but two of the most amazing women into my life. Both Lynda and Sue took me in and chose to love me as a mother loves a daughter. And they did it because they wanted to!

Honestly, I don't recall ever praying and asking for this. The Lord just decided to bless me with them! They saw the good in me and they believed in me. They loved, served, and cared for me and for my children. They have been there for weddings, funerals, showers, tragedies, joys, and even for the mundane in-between times, just like a mother would. And I get two of them!

They speak God's Word into my life and over me. They pray faithfully for my destiny and for the will of God for me. No one can replace my mother, but I am not alone and empty nor am I unloved. God used not one, but two willing servants to demonstrate His love and to help heal this orphan's heart. They taught me how to be a true mother in the faith and how to raise up both physical and spiritual daughters by the way they adopted me and gently and lovingly brought me up in my faith. The enemy tried to steal from me. Instead, God gave me a double blessing. I tearfully and humbly thanked The Lord for Lynda and Sue and all the love they poured into me.

That night, He also promised me a future harvest of orphaned souls. He said that the seed sown in sorrow will be cultivated in so much joy! I sat in my car, in a dark cemetery, a place of so much loss and rejoiced in the gain that is to come! I imagined the coming harvest of fellow 'orphans' in this world to whom I get to offer hope and healing to!

When I thought about it, I realized that every single one of us is born separated from our Heavenly Father, making us all orphans! We are born fatherless. If we are all born orphans, then there is no one who is not in need of The Love of The Father! Because I know the pain of being orphaned, I can speak to that need. I can tell others, I know what it feels like to be motherless and fatherless. And because of God's Love, I know what it feels like to be taken in and adopted by the Heavenly Father!

Psalm 27:10 says, "For my father and my mother have forsaken me, But the LORD will take me up." That has become my message to my children, to the women I minister to and to the world. This is how He planned to turn my mourning into dancing!

Yes, this is a grave I could dance on, even if the darkness was hiding it from me . . . *and, I'm positive my mom was dancing with me.*

The Fifth Grave

The Place Where You Grieved

My eye has also grown dim because of grief, And all my members are as a shadow.

—JOB 17:7

…then the days of weeping and mourning for Moses came to an end.

—DEUTERONOMY 34:8

*I*t was now day seven of the Feast and I had a big day ahead of me with four graves to go! I had the day off and planned to set out as soon as the kids left for school. Like the night before, my next stop was an actual grave, but this time, it was sunny and there was not a cloud to be seen. I thought to myself:

'It is a beautiful day for grave dancing, and I shouldn't have any trouble finding this one!'

When I arrived at the cemetery, the memories set in: the scene in my bathroom, the hospital, the funeral home, and the tiny casket. The memories seemed surreal and I felt a little strange driving into this cemetery. Probably because like my mom's death, I was at peace with this loss, too. I guess, when you drive into a cemetery to remember someone you loved and lost, you feel obligated to feel sad or mournful. I had already grieved, though, and was now comforted.

> I HAD NEVER MET HIM, EITHER, BUT I ALREADY LOVED HIM.

Driving in, I pictured the scene that beautiful warm summer day when my son, Colby, was laid to rest in that tiny casket. I was so blessed by the number of people who came to acknowledge the death of someone they had never met. I had never met him, either, but I already loved him.

I was sixteen weeks along in my tenth pregnancy when I began to feel contractions. I was laying in my bed on a typical Sunday morning. I asked my husband to get me some Tylenol because of the discomfort. I was a little worried. I needed to get up and get ready for church and the Tylenol helped the pain to subside. I got myself going and we left for church as we had to be there early to prepare for a special puppet show for the kids. As I was walking up the center aisle of the sanctuary, my water broke.

I was stunned.

I hadn't even considered the possibility of being in labor that morning.

I panicked and yelled for Doug.

He ran toward me and said, "What's wrong?"

I was crying and said, "My water broke! Take me home!"

I'm not sure why I said to take me home and not to the hospital. I still didn't even make the connection that I was in labor. I had miscarried once and given birth eight times already, but never this early; I was in shock.

When we arrived at home, I went straight to the bathroom. I brought the phone with me and called my doctor's office while I cried and tried to stay calm enough for them to understand me. They took my name and number and said a doctor would call me back. The doctor did call back – about two minutes after my son was stillborn in my bathroom.

> (If you have a weak stomach or have experienced anything like this, you may not want to read these next three paragraphs.)

I cried hysterically due to the trauma of having my son in the bathroom, on the toilet, and then to see him without life. I couldn't believe what just happened. At that moment, the phone rang, and the doctor tried to decipher what I was saying as I sobbed and sobbed. What followed was even harder to fathom.

FREE!

The doctor delicately told me it was crucial that I bring everything with me to the hospital. "I mean everything. The baby, the afterbirth, everything."

Doug came in the bathroom, took one look and broke down. He was as inconsolable as I was. I told him what the doctor had said, that we had to bring it all with us and go straight to the hospital. He left the bathroom for a moment and came back, still sobbing. He had a small Tupperware container and a large serving spoon. We had no medical instruments; we had no choice. Through tear-streaked eyes, sobbing together, we gathered up "everything" and transported our little one—who we would never know this side of Heaven— to the hospital. I held that container in my hands like I held my other eight babies in my arms.

(Continue reading for hope and encouragement.)

When we arrived at the hospital, we were greeted with gentleness and kindness; they were expecting us. We were assigned a nurse, an angel, really, that I will never forget. Her name was Claire. She loved God and she knew how to comfort hurting people. After I was examined and they determined that I was safe and okay, she asked us if we would like to see our baby. We were a bit confused. We had definitely already seen him, and then she explained. She offered to clean him up and present him to us in a way that would allow our memory of him to be tender, special, even dignified—unlike the way he was born.

We asked what she meant by cleaning him up and covering him. She explained what she meant patiently and carefully.

"Yes."

"Yes, we would like to see him."

When she left, Doug also stepped out of the room briefly. I found myself alone with God for the first time since it happened. I knew what I had to do. And I would do it sooner this time!

I miscarried my sixth pregnancy at eight weeks and felt very angry at God then. It took me a little while to recover spiritually from that. I felt betrayed, as if God didn't have my back. I stayed mad at God for a while after my first miscarriage, not knowing if I could trust Him and not understanding why He allowed such things to happen. I guess I blamed God.

> I FELT BETRAYED, AS IF GOD DIDN'T HAVE MY BACK. I GUESS I BLAMED GOD.

But I wasn't going to give the enemy that satisfaction again! No way; I wasn't falling for that trick. God does not create or delight in our loss, sorrow or suffering. He wants good things for His Children! He can hardly stand to watch us go through these things and only can because He knows He can heal any human heart of any wound. I know that now.

So, as soon as Doug stepped out, I said to the Lord, out loud, "Lord. I TRUST YOU. No matter what happens to me, I TRUST YOU. You are good!"

And there it was. I made it known—to myself, to my God, and to my enemy—what I believed, and that I would not be swayed by this tragedy.

Soon after, Doug returned and so did Claire. She had placed our baby in a little plastic soap dish and used a tiny square of gauze as his blanket. She presented him to us with a smile and announced, "It's a boy!" She then asked us if we had chosen any names and we told her yes, we had. She asked if there would be a funeral. She thought it would be appropriate to name him if we were going to have a funeral.

She has no idea how God used her to begin my healing process. She caused such a dramatic shift in the whole atmosphere of the situation. She did it with such love, the life-giving, tender, compassionate, honoring love of God. She validated all of our feelings while providing incredible comfort to our hurting hearts. She encouraged us to have a funeral and gave us resources to pursue when I was feeling better.

She was Heaven's ambassador sent for us.

When we got home, the emptiness set in. After a miscarriage, the physical emptiness is haunting. It's like even your body knows it's not supposed to be empty yet. Your whole being feels wrong. The physical feeling combined with the deep emotional sorrow over the loss were too much. The trauma of how it happened still had me in shock and I was sadder than I had ever been in my life. I was grieving and because of the suddenness and disturbing way it took place, I went into a deep place of sorrow. I lay on the couch and cried for days, as my heart ached.

Somehow, though the details were lost in the grief, a funeral got planned and was set for Friday. Each day that passed, more and more people dropped off food, delivered flowers, or sent cards.

At first, I thought, *'Oh, that's nice. Thank God I don't have to cook.'*

Friends would come with armloads of food and my sister, Kelly, came every day to feed my large family. I couldn't even get off of the couch because my heart was so sick.

I kept telling God how I hurt and how sad I was, but that I trusted Him and wasn't mad at Him. I reminded myself that His Word allows for a time of mourning and I told the Lord I would mourn until He said to rejoice. Each day, visitors brought more flowers, food, and cards. By Thursday, the house looked like a flower shop and I couldn't believe all of the love that physically surrounded me. I saw the Hand of my Father in all of it. Every effort to comfort me was from my Papa in Heaven.

> I KEPT TELLING GOD HOW I HURT AND HOW SAD I WAS.

I thought of Colby in Heaven with my mom. She's probably thrilled! Her favorite thing in life was being a grandmother. I started to see good with my spiritual eyes, but my heart was still sick.

The day of the funeral arrived, and I awoke to a strange feeling that something good was going to happen that day. I felt compelled to spend time with the Lord, in His Word and with my Journal.

He spoke to my heart. *'Today, your mourning has ended. Now rejoice in me!'*

Instantly, the heaviness of grief lifted off me, never to return. I rejoiced in this miracle and poured out my thanks for all of the comforting thoughts, words and prayers that flooded in that week. He then told me to 'comfort others with the comfort with which I was comforted.' And that's when I realized: I had just met The Comforter!

It is difficult to put into words the comfort that flooded my soul that day. It was like a million hugs and a warm blanket while being nursed back to health and having your back rubbed all at the same time. It flooded my soul and washed away my grief! I knew what I had to do.

I went to the funeral that day prepared to speak. The service was at the cemetery with the tiny casket as the focal point. A crowd of people circled the gravesite. My pastor spoke a few words and then asked if we had anything we'd like to say. I said, "Yes, I do."

> I WAS THANKFUL FOR MEETING THE COMFORTER.

I proceeded to tell our friends and family of my God, the God of all comfort. I told them that I was not thankful that I lost my son or for how it happened, but I was thankful for meeting The Comforter. Just as He introduced Himself as Healer, Deliverer, and Provider to the Israelites in the Wilderness, so did He in mine. I got a brand-new outlook on all of my suffering that day when He lifted the grief from my heart. None of it was wasted.

If I were never friendless, I wouldn't know Him as Friend. If I never wanted for anything, I wouldn't know Him as Provider. If I didn't need saving, I wouldn't know Him as Savior. If I never needed deliverance, I wouldn't know Him as Deliverer. And if I never grieved, I wouldn't know Him as Comforter.

I then shared this promise from Isaiah that He gave me that morning.

It became my greatest comfort when I thought of my son in Heaven.

> *"O afflicted one, storm-tossed, and not comforted,*
> *Behold, I will set your stones in antimony,*
> *And your foundations I will lay in sapphires.*
> *"Moreover, I will make your battlements of rubies,*
> *And your gates of crystal,*
> *And your entire wall of precious stones. "All your*
> *sons will be taught of the Lord;*
> *And the well-being of your sons will be great.*
>
> *"In righteousness you will be established;*
> *You will be far from oppression, for you will not*
> *fear; And from terror, for it will not come near you.*
>
> *"If anyone fiercely assails you it will not be from*
> *Me. Whoever assails you will fall because of you.*

> *"Behold, I Myself have created the smith who blows*
> *the fire of coals*
> *And brings out a weapon for its work; And I have*
> *created the destroyer to ruin.*
> *"No weapon that is formed against you will*
> *prosper; And every tongue that accuses you in judgment*
> *you will condemn.*
> *This is the heritage of the servants of the Lord,*
> *And their vindication is from Me," declares the*
> *Lord.*

—ISAIAH 54:11-17

Did you catch that? All of my sons would be taught of the Lord and great would be their well-being. All of them. And now I could say two of them are being taught and watched over in Heaven, directly by the Lord Himself! What more could a mother want for her children? Is there a better definition of well-being? I remembered how Hannah willingly offered her son, Samuel, to the Lord, to serve in His temple, and the peace and blessing she received. I, too, would willingly and joyfully offer my son to His Maker, without whom none of my children would exist.

I closed the service by thanking my faithful God for every facet of His nature and thanking my friends for all of their love and comfort. I haven't grieved since. That is why driving into the cemetery was surreal to me. I don't feel the pain of that experience any more.

I will tell you what I did feel while walking over to my son's little headstone on this grave hunting journey: frustration—again! You might not believe this, because I sure couldn't.

**I couldn't find his grave, either;
the place where I grieved.**

'This is just ridiculous, Lord! It's broad daylight! It's right here in the children's area by the statue of Jesus!'

I looked all over. It was nowhere! I was running out of time, too.

'Why in the world would I not be able to locate not one, but two actual graves?'

I struggled again with guilt. *'What kind of a mother cannot find her own son's grave?'*

Quickly, with His perfect peace settling on me, He drew me back in to His Heart.

'It is no accident that you could not find these graves. You couldn't find them because death has lost its sting in your life!'

I laughed out loud and marvelled at the stories Jesus writes in my life! Of course! The Lord knows how much I love symbolism. The graves were "gone" because there was no sting attached to them anymore. Brilliant.

> *1 Corinthians 15:55 says, "O death, where is your victory? O death, where is your sting?"*

Apparently, not there! I love how He works!

I made my way back to the car and began recording this revelation. It was sealed in my heart that my grief was ended and my heart was healed. As I wrote, I was overwhelmed with the reminder that, if I had not miscarried those two babies, I would have no Jonah and no Ella. Two of my precious blessings came just after each of those miscarriages. I imagined my life without them. *'Thank you, Lord, for Jonah and Ella! Their lives are a gift!'*

I don't have to understand the why to thank Him for the what . . . or the who . . . and I had a lot to be thankful for.

This is the grave where I grieved met The Comforter. Now I was equipped to comfort others. I promise anyone and everyone that when He says, "death has lost its sting," He means it. I look forward to the day when I will meet my two little precious dears in Heaven! In the meantime, I don't mind sharing them with Jesus and their beloved Grandma Leta.

I hopped in the car to head to the next place feeling alive, whole, and victorious! Five down. Three to go.

The Sixth Grave

The Place Where You Were Persecuted

Remember the word that I said to you, 'A
slave is not greater than his master.' If
they persecuted Me, they will also
persecute you

—JOHN 15:20

For what credit is there if, when you sin
and are harshly treated, you endure it
with patience? But if when you do what is
right and suffer for it you patiently
endure it, this finds favor with God.

—1 PETER 2:20

*I*t wasn't far to my next stop. I parked in front
of the church and thought about the irony
of a church being one of my graves. If you
know anything about the Word, you know

that being persecuted by religious people is not an uncommon experience. In fact, Jesus said, "if they did it to me, they'll do it to you." (John 15:20b)

It was the place I fellowshipped with the Lord and my church family for ten years. It was the church I was led to after I set my feet on the narrow road when I was twenty-one years old. I may have been an adult, but I was a baby Christian. I had no idea how to walk with God much less run my race. I was like a sponge; I couldn't get enough of the Word and I couldn't get enough truth. I went to almost every service, read books, and listened to tapes and CDs. I asked so many questions that I probably drove my pastor and his wife crazy.

Over the course of these ten years, I grew up in the Lord, grew in the Word, and eventually began to minister to other women through Bible studies and one-on-one counselling from the Word. I enthusiastically shared what I knew about God, although I had only just begun to scratch the surface.

It was during my years of participation in this ministry that I began to cry out to God to change me. I longed to be a better wife and mother. I was impatient and selfish, and I knew it. I began to devour book after book about marriage and child-training. I attended a book study led by the pastor's wife and the book was about being a godly wife. Throughout this study and beyond, I would ponder to myself, and even ask aloud, 'What do you do when your husband is doing something really wrong?'

We were told so many times by our Pastor's wife at these private meetings that it was dishonorable to say anything negative to anyone about our husbands, so I did not get specific about what he was doing wrong. I was so confused about what to do. Doug had stopped going to the bars to drink by this time, but there were still times I smelled alcohol on his breath or smelled marijuana in our basement. I wanted to do something about it, but I wanted so much to be a godly wife and please the Lord.

I finally got up the courage and asked my pastor's wife, "What do you do when your husband is doing something wrong that you know is wrong and you've asked him to stop, but he won't?"

The reply was simple and always the same. "You do not nag him. Talk to him about it once and if there is no change, then you trust the Lord to change him."

In addition to this very dangerous teaching, the elders of this church openly taught that 12-Step Programs and counselling were all "psycho-babble" and to be avoided. They said that all anyone needed was deliverance from The Lord.

If you have any experience with an addict, you're seeing the red flags pop up all over the place right now, as they should be! Confronting an addict with the truth only one time, and then remaining silent, is the equivalent of supplying them with the bottle or the pills or the pornography.

All I wanted to do was please the Lord and obey what I thought was His will. I was young, naïve about addiction, naïve about the Word, and I didn't do any further homework, though I should have. I respected this husband and wife, because their lives looked absolutely perfect from the outside. I later found out that she was doing exactly what it was that she was counselling me to do; she was an enabler, teaching others to enable.

Over time, I came to see that their lives only appeared perfect. There were a lot of red flags with him, their marriage and his leadership in the church. He was a very controlling husband and pastor. She practiced what she preached and I only saw her faithfully submit to him. She never complained or said words, or did anything that would appear to dishonor him.

I followed her example, believing wholeheartedly that this was my duty before the Lord. I trusted God with the whole mess and prayed that He would deliver my husband from chemical addiction. I made up my mind to "tell him once" and then not "nag" him about it.

You already know from that second grave that it didn't work. The hardest part for me was the talking to him only once . . . I was less than successful at this wrongful advice (ultimately for the better). I would go long stretches of time without saying anything and then I'd erupt like a volcano. He was isolating himself more and more, missing work more often, leaving me to take care of the kids and the house. But a godly wife trusts God with this, right? So, when I would erupt in anger, frustration, and fear for my family, his retort would be something about how I'll never be a godly wife because

I was too controlling. Guilt and condemnation would set in and I would end up repenting to God and begging my husband for forgiveness. I was being manipulated with what I thought was the truth about how to please God.

This pattern went on for the ten years that we attended that church. During that time, no one knew how bad Doug's addiction really was. *Not even me.* He was, like any addict, really good at covering it up or talking his way out of it when he got caught. Eventually, the truth comes out . . . and he was no exception.

The truth was exposed, suddenly and dramatically through a disastrous and potentially dangerous situation that Doug created with a man from church. Of course, it involved a night of illegal drugs and alcohol, so they both agreed that it would be best to keep it a secret. That didn't last long because the other man, a new convert, quickly felt guilty and confessed the whole thing to our pastor.

This is where it got interesting. Another pastor in leadership showed up at my doorstep and asked if he could talk to me. He lobbed question after question at me about Doug's behavior. He poked and prodded and pried until I told the truth about the previous ten years of Doug's addiction. I was so relieved! I carried it for so long by myself! I hated living in this prison of lies and fear. I was still scared, but at least the truth was known and I could finally say, out loud to my pastor, what was really going on! And I wasn't going around bad-mouthing my husband; I was simply answering my pastor's questions. Thank God! Or so I thought.

That's when I was blindsided.

He told me that I was in sin. He told me that covering up my husband's sin was no different than committing the sin myself and that I was equally as guilty in the eyes of God. He told me I should have been telling them all along and that I was a liar, too. He said I needed to repent, in front of the church. I was so confused!

The same church that taught me to submit to my husband and shut up about his mess was now accusing me of being a liar and an accomplice to his sin!

Then he delivered the final blow:

"No wonder your baby died."

I was crushed. Devastated. Completely confused. His words cut through my heart like a hot knife. My head swirled in pain, confusion, and fear.

'Was I the reason my son died?"

This question haunted me. It made me question who God is—is He really that guy? The one who kills babies because their mamas are foolish and sinful?

That is exactly what the enemy of my soul wanted me to think! Unfortunately for him, God and I went around this mountain once before. Remember? He doesn't take babies away from their mamas! He heals mama's hearts when Satan does, though. God is trustworthy because Jesus came to give life, not take it away.

The thief comes only to steal and kill and destroy; I
came that they may have life, and have it abundantly.

—JOHN 10:10

God and I settled the question of who I could trust
and who I couldn't when I lost both of my babies. This
was yet another attempt of Satan's to trick me into
blaming God and seeing Him as some kind of cruel
monster. And I was not having it.

We decided to visit another church the next Sunday
morning. When that same pastor found out that we
visited another church, he came to my house and
rebuked me. He told me not to follow my husband's
spiritual leadership anywhere.

He brought a stack of Bible verses that were
supposed to prove to me that I should stay in *his church*
and that I was only required by God to submit to my
husband in matters of the household and sexual
relations because he was in rebellion against God. He
said my husband was unrighteous and that I was under
no obligation to follow him as the spiritual leader of my
family anymore.

I was even more confused now! I couldn't imagine
a single one of the wives of the elders practicing the
advice this one was giving me! I sat under the lead
pastor's wife's teachings for years and I promise you,
nothing like that had ever been taught. Not a chance!
Well, I guess it all came down to who you were talking

to: a man in leadership or one of their wives . . . or one of the other pastors, or? But, isn't God's Word supposed to be unchanging?

And I couldn't help but ask the obvious question, "Why was it so wrong to go and visit a Bible-preaching church with my husband?"

I just wasn't seeing it. So, I asked the question. That was not a good idea.

After the next Sunday Service, in the middle of the fellowship hall, my pastor yelled at me saying I needed to repent.

He said I was full of spiritual pride because, "HOW DARE I QUESTION HIM!"

He demanded that there was no way that the five men of the Elder Board could be wrong and one woman be right. His words dripped with disdain. He then informed me that all of the women in the church had already been warned to stay away from me and my teaching. He continued on until I ran away in tears. This man was like a father to me and like a grandfather to my children. How did we get to this point? I felt condemned, dirty, and ashamed.

All I could think about was, *'What does God think? Does He agree with these men?'*

How could all of my efforts, all of the silent suffering I did in my marriage to please God, actually position me for church discipline? Was this some kind of sick joke?

I went straight home and lay on my bedroom floor for three hours crying out to the God I had been trying so hard to please all of those years.

"Lord, tell me if I'm wrong!" I begged. "I will repent right now! I will do anything to just be at peace with you! Am I wrong? Was I wrong? Why am I so terribly confused?"

Finally, His reply came. It wasn't in the form of an answer, it would take years to sort the lies from the truth and discover how deceived I had been – by others, by the enemy and by myself.

But, for now, wave after wave of grace and love began washing over me as I lay on the floor in a puddle of my own tears. I was in His Presence now, washed and clean. He loved me! Accepted me. He wasn't mad at me. Whether I was right or they were right no longer mattered. God had my back. Peace prevailed and I arose knowing that, whatever wrong I did, aware or not, I was forgiven, I was loved, and I was in His Grace. He knew I would need that incredible assurance as an anchor in the storm to come because this was only the beginning.

The topic for the following Wednesday night service was: SUBMISSION, announced to me personally by my pastor during his unannounced visit to our home.

I was not only alluded to in the sermon . . .

I was mentioned . . .

by name . . .

from the pulpit . . .

in a sermon that was being recorded!

I was held up as an example of what NOT to do.

**No doubt I was at my sixth grave;
the place where I was persecuted.**

I opted not to go to that service; so, I only know this because he stopped over the very next morning to deliver the tape. It was accompanied by a rebuke for not being there when he told me in advance the sermon was meant for me. I sheepishly took the tape and said I'd listen to it.

Eventually I did, but the words didn't affect me like he had hoped, because I knew I was okay with God. I also reached out to a respected pastor of another church in the area, a Bible believing, God-honoring church, and asked to meet. At our meeting, I told him the backstory, and I was completely honest about my marriage and the addiction/enabler dysfunction that plagued it. I told him why I was being disciplined by my Elder Board and then I asked him to listen to the tape. When we met a second time, he was stunned. He could not believe the words spoken against me and my husband from the pulpit and on tape. He said he was so shocked that he had his wife listen to it, too. He said that, regardless of the question of submission at hand, my chances of ever being respected by anyone in that body of believers were slim to none. He said my growth in that church was sure to be stunted permanently.

Thank God for wisdom given at the right moment. I had never even thought about that. It was time for us to go. We left the church shortly thereafter. Before we did, in the midst of my confusion about the submission issue, I had to do one more thing. I sought out the counsel of the head pastor's wife – the one who mentored me as a wife and mother for all of those years.

She was the "perfect" wife and mother on the outside, but, by now, I had discovered she was riddled with insecurities on the inside. Nevertheless, I sought her counsel almost as if to prove to myself I heard her right all those years ago and to prove that I wasn't crazy. I asked her if it was indeed wrong for me to go to visit another church with my husband because he was in sin and unrighteous. Sure enough, she told me to follow my husband. She assured me that if he wasn't asking me to join a cult, but taking me to a Bible believing church, then there was nothing wrong with me following him there.

'I knew it!' I knew I heard her right all of those years. Furthermore, she could not explain to me why it was wrong that I did not expose his addiction for all of those years. She just didn't have an answer for why I was rebuked as a liar and an accomplice to his sin. She shook her leg nervously the whole time we spoke and was visibly uncomfortable with the whole conversation.

Ironically, three days later, she contacted me and

told me that she had talked with her husband (the lead pastor) about our conversation. She apprehensively explained to me that she was wrong three days earlier. She said she should have consulted her husband and the Scriptures first. She needed to set the record straight. She was now advising that I should not, in fact, follow my husband to another church. I should not follow his spiritual leadership anywhere. Wow. What a strange way to get the confirmation I needed.

Over time and with a lot of studying, I discovered that I was taught incorrectly what Godly submission really is. The elders of my church at that time taught their wives a slave-like submission, which I attempted to emulate. The women praised me for it and then the men in leadership penalized me for it – for not exposing my husband and rejecting him as my spiritual leader. How confusing and misleading!

They were right about God not wanting me to be an enabler. That is true. I needed to confront, and set boundaries, and shine some light on our dark places, but I am fairly confident that they would have never tolerated it if their wives did the same!

Why? Because they were "men of God" and my husband was not. The fact of the matter is, whether your husband is a pastor or a prisoner, submission does not equal turning a blind eye to controlling behavior, including the controlling behaviors of those who are supposed to be spiritual leaders.

Women are not called to slave-like submission to our husbands or to God. We are free to choose to submit and a woman will do that if she is loved with Christ's Love, which is sacrificial and selfless. If you are enabling a controlling, manipulative, or addicted husband in the name of obedience to the Word of God, that is not submission and that is not what God requires of you.

Doctors Henry Townsend and John Cloud, authors of Boundaries in Marriage, say it best:

"Whenever submission issues are raised, the first question that needs to be asked is: what is the nature of the marital relationship? Is the husband's relationship with his wife similar to Christ's relationship with the church? Does she have free choice, or is she a slave "under the law"?

"Many marital problems arise when a husband tries to keep his wife "under the law," and she feels all the emotions the Bible promises the law will bring: wrath, guilt, insecurity, and alienation (see Romans 4:15; Galatians 5:4). I have never seen a "submission problem" that did not have a controlling husband at its root. When the wife begins to set clear boundaries in marriage, the lack of Christlikeness in a controlling husband becomes evident, because the wife is no longer enabling his immature behavior. She is confronting the truth and setting biblical limits on hurtful behavior. Often, when the wife sets boundaries, the husband begins to grow up."

Thankfully, God holds us accountable for what we know, when we know it. He looks at our deepest motives and, although I was misguided, I desired to please Him and He saw my desire. He saw my heart. I practiced that unhealthy, slave-like submission, believing it would please God. And I believe it did please Him. How could it, you might ask. Because man looks at the outer appearance, but God looks at the heart. (2 Samuel 16:7b) But He was just as pleased when I sought spiritual guidance that honored Biblical submission, a chosen submission to love and freedom.

He showed me a word picture representing how He sees our attempts at Godly living, especially as baby Christians: It is much like when your three-year-old wants to surprise you with breakfast in bed. When you are awakened by her little sweet voice, you open your eyes to find a tray filled with raw eggs, spilled juice, cereal overflowing with too much milk, and no silverware to eat any of it! When you get to the kitchen, the mess is even worse. But, oh, how sweet her little face is all lit up with that look-what-I-did-for-you-Mommy smile.

Well, this is what God gets to "wake up to" every day with His children. In a way, we are all His messy kids, learning to make less of a mess as we mature. I am no exception. As the perfect Father that He is, He meets our Here-you-go-Daddy-I-made-something-just-for-you attempts with grace and mercy. There's no berating, no lecture, and no punishment. He allows us to learn from the natural consequences of our actions, shows us how to clean up the messes we made, and continues to gently teach us exactly how to make that breakfast.

As I sat parked in front of my old church, I realized that's exactly what He did for me. He had redeemed it all. He taught me how to make breakfast. Thank you, Lord!

This confusing time of being publicly persecuted for how I lived out my faith was actually a gift to me. The confusion and pain of this circumstance compelled me to dig into God's Word like I never had before and "study to show myself approved." (2 Timothy 2:15) I searched the scriptures to find out what God said about submission, marriage, godliness, and church leadership. I asked for wisdom and discernment. I took ownership of the fact that I chose to believe what was taught—blindly—and I prayed that God would make me wiser for it in the years to come.

This philosophical difference also compelled me to seek counsel from other church leaders who had no ties with mine. I heard such wise and practical counsel for the first time in a decade. I realized I had only heard one view from one source for so long, I no longer recognized false teaching when I heard it.

In short, my farewell experience with this church and its leaders was a catapult into maturity and knowledge of the Word, but not for the reasons they had hoped. It was also the reason I decided, no matter where we go to church, I was not keeping Doug's addiction a secret ever again!

I told Doug we needed help and would only get it if we asked for it. There would be no surprises at the new church.

I had my opener all prepared: *'Hi! We're Doug and Kim and we are a complete mess! He's an alcoholic and I'm an enabler. Nice to meet you!'*

Sigh; there's freedom in the truth! Praise God for revealing what was hidden, no matter how painful it was.

My spiritual mom, Sue, always says, "No matter how much it hurts, the truth is always your friend."

The truths that this grave revealed have served me well, just like a dear friend would. Although I received bad counsel, I am also responsible for my choices and I chose to take that counsel and did not do my own homework.

I am careful to consider many opinions and dig into the Word before I take counsel now. Another truth that has served me well is that I must forgive those in leadership who persecuted me, misled me, manipulated me, or wronged me in anyway. This was hard to do, because of the high standard we hold people in ministry to and because many of the hurtful things done to me were done in the Name of The Lord. Yes, they will be held to a higher account by God, but we must remember that men and women in church leadership are still just that—men and women. They are flawed and will fail us.

Ultimately, their sins are between them and God. What matters most is that I forgive them. I forgive because I need to be forgiven. (Matthew 6:14)

> **I FORGIVE BECAUSE I NEED TO BE FORGIVEN.**

The greatest pearl I received from this grave is this: I understand what God requires of me when His Word tells me to submit to my husband and other authorities. I understand how to honor and respect, while still setting boundaries around hurtful behavior. I know how to take a stand for righteousness, instead of being a slave to controlling authority. What a relief!

My friend, if you are going to be a true disciple of Christ, you should expect to be persecuted by other Christians in some way, for something. Jesus said that if He was, then we would be, too. We must resist the temptation to be offended and instead we should pass this test like Jesus did.

"Father, forgive them, for they know not what they do."

—Luke 23:34

I uttered those very words as I sat looking at the church building that was grave number six. I treasured all the truths revealed to me there. They were now cemented into my character forever, like jewels in a crown. Thank you, Jesus for making this grave a dance floor, too!

FREE!

The Seventh Grave

The Place Where You Failed

"Failure is undeniable evidence that you are making progress toward your goal."

— ANDREA WALTZ, GO FOR NO!

Truly, truly, I say to you, unless a grain of wheat falls into the earth and dies, it remains alone; but if it dies, it bears much fruit.

—JOHN 12:23

When God told me to make this one of my stops, it definitely made sense to me. I knew why. This was a place where you could say something died. It was the place that confirmed one of my worst fears . . . that I was, in fact, a failure. This was the beautiful office that housed memories of my first attempt at a career that did not involve laundry, dishes, and wiping butts.

FREE!

Launching a new career is always challenging, but even moreso when you are a single mom of eleven kids and you've been out of the game for years. Nevertheless, I was excited and I needed to do it! I wasn't just going to work a job; I was going to be a businesswoman with a real career. I didn't know how else I could financially support my kids and get us to a better place and it was all I could think about.

The thought of me as a successful career woman with the bank account to show it made the dream I had since I was little come alive in me. I always wanted to be just like my dad – a successful businessman and entrepreneur.

My new job would be at my friends, John and Sue's financial advisory firm. John worked in the financial industry for a very long time and had more knowledge in his pinky than I had in my whole body. He knew my situation, my strengths, and my weaknesses . . . and he believed in me. In fact, they were both convinced I was the perfect woman for the job. They invited me to join the firm as a Client Advocate Representative. My role would be to promote the firm and bring in new clients so that the advisors could do the advising. Their confidence in me made me confident. I believed that this time would be different. By different, I meant that I would NOT fail as I usually did with new ventures. I never had an opportunity like this before. And this time, I had to succeed.

In my early years of adulthood, I had attempted several direct sales businesses with the promise of success. Everyone always told me I was "perfect" for it and that I would be a huge success. I got my hopes up and they were always dashed when customers were not beating down my door and blowing up my phone to buy my products. After several tries and never finding success, I concluded that I was destined to be a failure. On paper I was. I failed at marriage, I failed at business, I failed at motherhood (that's another whole book). I tried and failed and tried and failed. I started to believe there was something about me that just could not be successful.

In a way, I was right, but it was my thinking—based on a lie—that held me back, not my actual ability. My fear of failure and rejection, along with limiting beliefs about what I was capable of, just didn't set me up for success.

I didn't know that those were my obstacles yet, but I did know that I had the love and support of two of the most generous, loving people you could meet, John and Sue. I borrowed their confidence in me, gratefully accepted their support, and I began working at their firm.

In four months, while single parenting ten of my kids, ages two to seventeen, and working as the firm's receptionist, I studied and passed three rigorous, mind-numbing, financial industry tests. This allowed me sell investments and securities in order to make a commission. I also became licensed in the state of Wisconsin to sell life, accident, and health insurance by passing that test, too.

Once legit, I could make commissions by bringing new people into the firm. When they became clients, I got paid. It sounded great and it sounded easy. The earning potential was certainly huge and I believed I would get there. So did John. He even told me that I was going to be so successful I would become the poster child for single mothers everywhere. He said I was going to be on Oprah. Sounded great to me! Everyone loves a good underdog story. After all the kids and I had been through, I wouldn't mind being one!

As an independent contractor with the firm, my success was up to me. *This is the crux of why I failed.* As right as John was about how well I worked with people and how my personality was perfect for sales, he missed something. In fact, I missed it too. I didn't actually discover it until after this manuscript was started! Because of my past, I was terrified of the word, "NO." I equated the word "no" in business to personal rejection. And if you are afraid of a no, there is one sure fire way to avoid hearing it.

Don't ask.
Don't ask for a yes, and you will never hear a no.

Do you know any successful salespeople who got that way by NOT asking anyone to buy their product or service? Me neither. I knew I would not succeed unless I actually set meetings and invited people to come into the firm, but I just couldn't bring myself to do it. I was comfortable talking to close friends, but most of my close friends were not candidates for the firm. I had a mental block when it came to approaching aquaintances and completely froze at the thought of cold calling. My fear of failure and my fear of rejection plucked out any confidence that had taken root.

I began to question what I was doing. In addition to my own internal obstacles, the economy posed its own. I passed my last test in July of 2008, right before the Stock Market crash on 9-11. Most people were afraid to touch their money, much less move it to a new firm after the huge losses they incurred. I told myself this wasn't the timing or the job for me. This excuse was a whole lot easier than facing my fears, especially since I didn't even know that my fears were the real reason I was holding myself back.

I brought two or three new clients into the firm and continued to work as the firm's receptionist. While I was there, I observed John living his passion and purpose. The more I watched John running his business, passionately talking to others about financial matters, and tirelessly looking for more and better ways to protect people's wealth, the more I realized that the financial industry, no matter how interesting, would never be my passion.

This realization fueled my desire to live my own purpose and fulfill my destiny. It didn't just create a hunger in me; it brought me to a decision-making point.

Would I go forward or would I walk away?

While I was deliberating, the state informed me that they would no longer pay for daycare unless my sales postion produced an income. Fair enough, but that meant I had no daycare for three little ones if I continued to struggle with this job. By this time, instead of my dream of becoming a successful businesswoman, I had to start taking cleaning jobs to pay my bills. Cleaning was the perfect way to make good money in a short time, get paid immediately, and be in control of my schedule, so I could be there for my kids. The state did pay for daycare for that. It was time for me to let go of the struggle, accept my failure, and do what I needed to do to take care of my family.

I was at my seventh grave; the place where I failed.

When my first major career attempt failed, I reasoned, 'I failed, so I must be a failure.'

Makes sense, right? I beat myself up over it, for a bit, but the overwhelming sense of relief when the pressure was removed would overrule my feelings of guilt and failure. I knew wholeheartedly that I had no passion for the financial industry and that my future was not going to be found there.

With that said, I still couldn't shake the idea of my future in the business world. What was my passion? How could it translate to a business that produced enough income for my large family? I believed there was an answer. I knew I was called to help people and I knew I would one day write and speak. God put that dream in my heart all the way back in my twenties. But how in the world would this girl ever finish anything much less finish it successfully? I couldn't see it because it had never happened for me.

I KNEW I WAS CALLED TO HELP PEOPLE.

During my time at the firm, the Lord spoke many times, through many sources, telling me I was destined to succeed in business, even while I was failing there. One prophet, a stranger to me, told me I would be wildly successful. He said the Lord would give me an idea that would make me very wealthy if I obeyed Him and followed His lead.

John, Sue, and Lynda spoke of their belief in me constantly. They said I was a leader with an anointing to minister to people in the marketplace. They spoke of my future success frequently and even announced it to others when they would introduce me. (No pressure, right?) They told me I was wired for success and created to thrive in business. Slowly, I came to believe it. I saw myself the way they and God saw me. I envisioned my future as a successful business woman, and it looked good!

I held onto each word, idea, thought, dream, and vision and believing it would come to pass. I began to see myself as a success, a leader, and a person of influence. I craved the day I would thrive, not just survive. As the vision of my future success grew inside me, I was working as a house cleaner for already-successful people. I would daydream and plot my business plans while cleaning their toilets. I believed with all my heart that my day would come if I obeyed the Lord. Some days, I washed their floors with my tears. After all, if you have to be down on your knees, you might as well pray.

As I drove up to the firm that day, it was less than a year after leaving it. A familiar feeling settled in as I found a parking space. The sights and sounds reminded me of my time there and my attempt at success. I felt satisfied with myself for passing all those difficult exams and for surviving a three-day insurance seminar! (Anyone who has ever done that deserves tons of credit.)

I thought of how much I loved putting on my business clothes and how much God had changed me since I was in the working-world fourteen years earlier, before I began homeschooling my kids. I knew who I was now, and I was actually okay with it! Even though this venture failed, I knew where I was headed. I daydreamed yet again about my future success and what God might have me do. I knew my destiny was sealed in Him.

I sat staring at the logo on the entrance door.

"What was it all for, Lord? There is purpose in everything when we follow your voice, even when we fail, so what was the purpose?"

His answer came through loud and clear. "Rejoice, Daughter! Unless a grain of wheat falls into the earth and dies, it remains alone; but if it dies, it bears much fruit. You will bear more fruit in the marketplace than you can imagine!"

Isn't that just like my God to bring forth new life from death? I was sitting in front of my seventh grave that week realizing that I was poised for an incredible resurrection. I had planted a tiny seed and it surely died there. It appeared that nothing came from all my efforts or all that John and Sue invested in me . . . if you only looked at the surface!

There was fruit, a harvest inside of me and another kind of harvest to come. I was changed and, one day, through my business, God promised I would be an agent of change.

FREE!

The Lord began to show me pictures in my mind and heart of all that I gleaned from my time at the firm. In part, my time there was a door that was flung wide open for me to make many new connections. I met people there that are still in my life today, and are continuing to connect me with new people. Each connection, each door has brought me closer to fulfilling my destiny. The firm wasn't my destination, but it was a critical stop along the way.

In addition, He used that time to mold me into someone new. It was there, in an industry full of wealthy men that this impoverished single woman with a bunch of kids was forced to "rub elbows" with them. This may sound silly, but God knew I needed that! If you can't even be around successful, wealthy people without being nervous and insecure, how are you ever going to be one?

Let me draw you a picture of my "portfolio," when I started at the firm. My life was riddled with financial struggle from the time my dad left until the moment I stepped foot into the firm. I had lived the majority of my life with very little, feeling inferior to others. When I started working for John, I was a single mom of ten, ages two to seventeen. I was on welfare and received food stamps, health insurance, and daycare from the state. It was 2008 and the only vehicle I owned was a 1995 Ford Clubwagon fifteen passenger van that was given to me. I lived in a one-hundred-year old farmhouse that was in an extreme state of disrepair, to put it mildly. My ex-husband had only paid me two months of child support since the separation and, at the time of his departure, we were behind on all the bills with no savings. I walked into the firm a statistic. I was "that woman." I was the poor, struggling, visiting-the-food-pantry, please-won't-you-sponsor-my-children-for-Christmas, thankful-for-any-help-I-could-get woman. I went to those financial classes and testing centers wondering what people would think if they knew who I really was. I said little and kept mostly to myself.

But something happened to me when thrust into direct contact with successful men and women. I began to see myself as one of them. After all, I was in their world now and they were people, just like me. I discovered that some struggled as much as I did and some, even more. They were all wounded in some way and they all sinned just like me. That, in my opinion, put us all in the same boat. What was strangest to me was finding that I had something that they didn't. I had an intimacy with Christ because of my Wilderness that made me the wealthiest woman in the room, no matter what room I was in. I knew God. He had even shared some of His treasures from the deep with me! How could I see myself as poor? I learned that the Love of God knows no bounds, no classes, no wealth, and no poverty because everybody needs it. I slowly discovered that, in the ways that mattered, I was the successful one.

I started to carry myself differently. Even when I was cleaning toilets, shaking rugs, scrubbing a floor, or vacuuming, I didn't carry myself as a cleaning lady. Sure, I was there to serve, but I wasn't a second-class citizen. I wasn't "less than," anymore. In fact, I carried myself as a business owner. I did, after all, own a cleaning business! I even daydreamed of someday hiring some employees other than my kids! (I'm sure they dreamed of that, too!) I ran my business and loved the families I cleaned for. The dream in my heart to own a business and succeed was planted there by God and he promises never to put to shame those who trust in Him.

As I sat in front of that office, I smiled. This failure didn't sting anymore. In fact, it wasn't a failure at all. I knew that it was a necessary stepping stone to teach me something I needed to know for the next leg of the journey. Because of my experience there, I am not who I was! I came to see my future self with new eyes and today, I am walking in that newness.

Since then, I've even come to redefine failure completely. Failure isn't a person, it's an event! You see, there is not one successful person that can say he or she has never failed. *Not one.*

Failure is part of the human experience. Some people say that, if you're not failing frequently, you must not be doing much! I've come to look at failure simply as bricks on the road to my destiny. That road is made up of bricks representing success and bricks represening failure. Some say yes and some say no. Together, they are the perfect path to my destiny. I will get there as long as I don't quit!

The seed of destiny is a seed God Himself planted inside of me. He planted it inside of you, too. We want that seed to take root and shoot straight up! We mistakenly think that all will go right and that a beautiful flower will bloom with ease. But Jesus said that, in order for any seed to grow and produce fruit, it must first be buried in the dirt and die.

Truly, truly, I say to you, unless a grain of wheat falls into the earth and dies, it remains alone; but if it dies, it bears much fruit.

—John 12:24

Failure serves as the grave where you can bury your seed of destiny! If you accept your failure as an event (not your identity) and find the treasures hidden in it, your seed will bear much fruit! I know mine has.

God has been so faithful to me allowing me to fulfil my purpose in Christ in business! I am grateful for all of those houses I cleaned, but I am not a house cleaner anymore.

Instead, I'm privileged to empower women to live extraordinary lives and tell their stories. I do this through my natural health business, through the Fellowship of Extraordinary Women (FEW), and through FEW International Publications.

FEW was always my destiny. Everything I experienced led me to founding that organization and prepared me for it; my business ventures that did not work out, as well as my days spent serving others by cleaning their toilets.

I believe that women were created to be an answer for the problems we face in our world today. And I am on a mission to make women all over the world believe that, too. We can be an answer when we understand our true identity in Christ and embrace our God-given destiny! When women believe that everywhere they go, with the power of God, they can be a part of the solution, there is no way they cannot live an extraordinary life!

Now, because of FEW, women are stepping into their purposes for God, and confidently using their gifts to make so many positive impacts. With boldness they are arising as leaders because of the sisterhood of FEW and of FEW Authors. Relationships, friendships, connections, and wisdom are flowing from these circles of women as each woman calls the other higher! I have watched as these extraordinary leaders have: improved the physcial, spiritual and mental health of those in their communities, reached out to and encouraged fellow cancer survivors, guided those who've been abused to victory, empowered female entrepreneurs to greatness, infused mothers with the courage to lead, and expanded one another's faith in the power of God's Word—in their own circles and even around the world.

I'm so blessed! And the seed I laid to rest in a financial office and offered to God is now a blessing to women around the globe! I hold to the Promise of God that says I will bless and serve many more. (Isaiah 43:5-6) Only God can cause the beauty of new life to spring up from a cold dark grave. That is how God writes stories!

That's how this grave became a garden.

The Eighth Grave

The Place Where You Sacrificed

After these events, God tested and proved Abraham...

— Genesis 22:1

For now I know that you fear and revere God, since you have not held back from Me...

—Genesis 22:12

I't's funny. As I opened my journal to make my final stop, I discovered that my pen would be making the first marks in a brand-new section of my notebook. A new beginning for the final grave. That was so fitting for this particular story! In fact, it is the theme of this chapter. It was time to visit the eighth grave and the number eight represents new beginnings!

I love how nothing is random with God.

This grave was the burial place of the new, wonderful beginning that I chose to sacrifice. It was the place where God asked me to offer back to Him my dream of loving and being loved, and I said, "Yes."

As I parked my car and took in the view at grave number eight, I had beautiful memories to match the beautiful scenery. It was a warm, sunny day on the Lake Michigan shoreline, much like the day when this lovely, romantic spot became a gravesite in my life. This grave was pretty fresh. I had been there earlier that month with the one I had fallen in love with two and a half years before. The one I loved more than any other. The one who loved me like no other.

Our story began in 2008. My eighteen-year marriage was over, and the kids and I were both scared and excited about our new life. I was working up to five jobs at one point to keep us afloat while Doug was in and out of jail, prison, or treatment and child support was wishful thinking.

During this time, I found my strength in God's love for me. I spent many hours in prayer and worship. Any chance I got, alone in my car, alone in the bathroom, alone in my bedroom at night, I was with the Lord. He spoke to me often and with great grace and incredible mercy. He promised me healing and He pledged his faithfulness to me. He assured my heart many times that He is a father to the fatherless. I trusted Him with everything that I could not do for myself and for my children . . . which was a lot . . . most things, in fact. I was so physically tired at the end of each day that I fell into bed at night. I cried myself to sleep often, not from fear or despair, but because of absolute exhaustion. The kids at home were between the ages of two and seventeen. My baby was still in diapers and I had four teenagers, not to mention the five in between. I was spread so thin you could see through me. Yet, I was positive that God's promises would not return void for my family.

> I AWOKE EXPECTANT. I SENSED THAT SOMETHING GOOD WAS GOING TO HAPPEN TODAY.

During the Spring of 2008, my prayers and time with God led me to a three-day fast. I was instructed to fast, as Esther did, and to read one chapter of Esther each of the three days beginning with chapter three. I knew this fast was ordained by God, because I do not like fasting and I did this one with ease. I had no appetite or desire for food. On the third day, I awoke expectant. I sensed that something good was going to happen today.

I got up and went to work as usual, but received a call from one of the kids' schools. I had to leave work early and go take care of something. That put me at home, alone, in the middle of the afternoon, for the first time in a very long time. I felt the Lord drawing me to Himself.

FREE!

I opened my Bible to Esther, Chapter 5, and my heart was pierced by these words:

On the third day [of the fast] Esther put on her royal robes and stood in the royal or inner court of the king's palace opposite his [throne room]. The king was sitting on his throne, facing the main entrance of the palace.

And when the king saw Esther the queen standing in the court, she obtained favor in his sight, and he held out to [her] the golden scepter that was in his hand. So Esther drew near and touched the tip of the scepter.

Then the king said to her, What will you have, Queen Esther? What is your request? It shall be given you, even to the half of the kingdom.

—ESTHER 5:1-3

What did this mean to me? What was God trying to tell me? Could it be that He was telling me what King Xerxes told Esther?

Was my King, the King of Kings, extending His Golden Scepter to me? Was He, in fact, telling me to ask for anything, even up to half of his Kingdom, and that He would grant it to me? His Presence and this question put me on the floor.

As I lie there trembling and sobbing, I knew I was at a moment of destiny in my life. I did not know when or if I would have this opportunity again. I first thanked Him for His incredible favor and generous Spirit. I then thought long and hard. I did not want to waste this opportunity on trivial matters. I could ask for anything! What should I ask for? I remembered two wise people. The first was Solomon who asked for wisdom when he was told he could have anything.

Like King Solomon, I prayed "Lord, give me wisdom to lead your people." Then I asked for knowledge and understanding.

Next, I considered Joyce Meyer's wisdom when she said, "I'd rather ask God for everything and receive some of it than ask God for nothing and receive all of it."

So, I did it. *I asked him for everything.* I asked him to enable me to fulfil my destiny. I asked Him to provide for my children. I asked Him to make us a family that brings Glory to Himself. I asked Him for the love of a faithful husband and for a father for my children. I prayed that my children would each fulfil their destinies in Christ and that they would be totally healed and restored. I then asked Him for every one of my heart's desires.

I asked to reach people around the world with God's message.

I asked to be a hope dealer on every continent.

I asked to be successful in ministry.

I asked God to allow me to show Him to people of influence with large platforms.

I asked for a home that my whole family could return to as a refuge, no matter how large our family gets.

I asked to be able to give my children the things I couldn't provide when they were young . . . the cars, the vacations, the memories that once made me content as a child; the life that I always felt they deserved.

I asked to have the resources to be able to give so big that I could change a life with just one gift.

After all, God gave us the one gift that changed my life . . . His Son.

I poured it all out and laid it at His feet until I couldn't think of anything else. And then I waited. I waited, and I listened.

"It is Finished."

"It is finished? It is finished, Lord? That means yes... to everything? Yes to wisdom, yes to provision, yes to love, yes to my heart's desires?"

I felt His Golden Scepter was right there for me to touch. He made me feel like Esther herself! I put on worship music and worshiped my King right there on the floor for a long time.

In the days that followed, the Lord kept telling me that it was going to happen fast. I sensed it. I'd wake up in the morning and say, "It could be today."

What was this "it?" It was really a "him." I knew I was going to meet the one I prayed for, the one God said yes to. I just didn't think it would be so soon after He said yes.

About a month after the fast, I was leaving church with my youngest six kids. I discovered that they were out in the parking lot swarming some guy's Harley-Davidson motorcycle and Eli, my son who was only three and a half, was climbing all over it.

With two-year-old Ava, my youngest, in my arms, I ran out to the parking lot to retrieve all of them, (especially Eli) to spare this man's chrome and paint job.

"Kids, what are you doing? You need to get away from that motorcycle. Eli, get down from there!"

The man assured me that he gave my son permission to be on the bike, but I removed him anyway.

"Oh, thank you, but no. Kids, we have to get going," I instructed.

The man added, "To a birthday party! Right?"

I thought, "Well that's strange. The kids must have told him."

"Yes," I replied, "that's right."

To which he added, "To your sister's house in Elkhorn, right?"

I wondered whether the kids gave him my social security number and blood type, too.

"Come on, kids! We don't want to be late. Let's go."

As I walked back to my van, I thought I may have been somewhat abrupt, so over my shoulder I said, "By the way, my name is Kim. It was nice to meet you."

He yelled to my back as I continued walking away, "I'm glad to meet you, Kim. I'm Scott. I've been wanting to meet you for a while now."

What? What was that supposed to mean!? Was this guy hitting on me? I got all the kids gathered together in the van, closed the doors and got out of the parking lot as fast as I could. I wasn't sure how I felt about his statement, 'I've been wanting to meet you'.

Had he been watching me? Flattering . . . or creepy. I couldn't decide. I was intrigued and bothered at the same time. We attended the same church, but I hadn't noticed him before.

On the way to the party, the kids said to me, "Mom, he's so nice. You should really go out with him."

In a motherly tone I said, "Kids, I just met him in the parking lot. It's really not wise to go out with someone you just met."

"But he's so nice, Mom, and he's going to bring us shark teeth and pictures of dolphins next week."

"Really?" is what I said, but, *'Ha!'* is what I thought. "We'll see if he brings shark teeth and dolphins."

In my experience, you were wise NOT to believe things that men told you. We went off to the party and I was mercilessly teased about this Harley-riding man from church by my whole extended family. I assured them "It's not going to happen."

I had already determined that the biker was not worthy of my trust.

The next week, as soon as church let out, my kids flew back out to that parking lot looking for the Harley and the guy who went with it. They found it and they found Scott. Sure enough, he produced the shark teeth and the pictures of dolphins. I was legitimately surprised. The kids came running to get me as I left the church to show me their new treasures.

"Mom! Mom! Look! Come and see the pictures of the dolphins! Look at these shark teeth! Aren't they cool?"

I thought that was nice, but it would take a lot more than some shark teeth and dolphins to impress me! You've got to remember I met my first husband in church, too. Scott could have had a white collar on and I would've been a skeptic.

His son, Nick, and my son, Jonah, ran around together for a while. They were both eleven and had met in Children's Church. After all the excitement wore down a little bit, I took a break from judging Scott and thanked him for the nice gesture of the shark teeth and dolphin pictures. I told him how much my kids love animals and then I started to make motions to leave.

His response was, "Oh! Your kids love animals? Well, Nick and I love animals, too! Would you ever want to go to the zoo and hang out, maybe? I could, um, give you my number and um, we could maybe plan something."

My chin fell to the parking lot and my eyes popped out of my skull involuntarily. He knew in an instant that something about that idea didn't sit well with me. He leaned forward and said sincerely, "I'm so sorry. Did I just offend you?"

My response was simply, "Uh . . . yeah!" (I wanted to day, *'DUH!'*)

He nervously said, "Oh! Well, then there will be no phone number and no zoo . . . come on, Nick! It's time to go. Have a really nice day. We'll see you later." Now he was the one making a beeline for it.

I couldn't believe he asked me to the zoo right in front of the kids. What a position he put me in! Now, if

I said no, I'm crushing them. Nice. Plus, I hadn't been asked to hang out with a man since I was seventeen years old and that was nineteen years ago! It was just plain awkward all the way around!

The kids and I scurried to the van while he and Nick got on his Harley and began to drive away. What I wasn't telling the children was that seeing him with his son on the back of his Harley each week was starting to get to me. You rarely see that. You see a lot of guys with their "babes" on the back of their bikes, but very few with a son. I wanted to watch them ride away. I thought it was sweet.

I quietly said to the kids, "I kind of want to watch them leave."

As they left, we left, too, and as God and bad timing would have it, we ended up at the same intersection a minute later, them turning right, us turning left. Him, on his Harley, me, driving my big red bus.

My son, Jonah, decided then would be a good time to roll his window down and tell Scott what I said.

"Hey! My mom said she wants to watch you ride away!"

Ahhh! I was mortified! Scott made sure to make eye-contact and smile at me, so I quickly rolled up the window and leaned back in my seat so that he couldn't see my face turn red. And off they rode.

On the drive home, I had the chance to be mortified again, but this time by my kids' latest suggestion.

"He was so nice. You shouldn't just date him, Mom, you should marry him."

"Marry him?" I exclaimed, "I don't even know what he does for a living!"

The kids were happy to volunteer that information. "Oh, Mom, don't worry. We know what he does! He drives a semi. He's a truck driver."

I stared incredulously in my rear-view mirror at all of their faces.

"He's a truck driver? He's a truck driver." Great. "Okay kids. Listen carefully. This guy is a trucker for a living who rides a Harley for fun. There is no way that he is not on something or in recovery. We are done with that life. We're not going back! For anyone. No matter how nice they are. So just forget about this guy, okay?"

One sweet little voice chimed in, "Mommy? What's recovery?"

"Never mind, Sweetie."

Another began to plead with me, "But Mom! We really like him. He's so nice!"

"I'm sure he's lovely when he's sober. Now we are done talking about this." I stated.

That was the end of that.

Their response to him really concerned me. I was NOT cool with my children giving their hearts away to a stranger in a church parking lot! It broke my heart that they were so hurting, lonely, and desperate for a father figure that they would give their hearts so quickly and so freely. I knew all too well where that could get them!

I decided it was time for me to have a talk with this Harley stranger. Next Sunday, I would pull him aside and I would kindly, but firmly, explain to him what our situation was and lay down some serious ground rules. You don't want to mess with a grizzly momma! I was the only one left to protect my kids.

The following Sunday came, and it was Mother's Day. As part of my Mother's Day gift, my oldest children, who had stopped going to church some time before that, informed me that they would be attending church with me as part of my gift. I was excited to have all eleven of my kids with me in church and was feeling so loved! That is, until I remembered that my house was more like a high school and that word travelled fast.

"Wait a minute." I said to the older kids. "You guys aren't coming to church as a gift to me, you just want to check out the Harley-Trucker, don't you?"

They laughed mischievously and nodded.

When the Mother's Day service let out, before I could collect my Bible and my purse, they were gone. I discovered all eleven of my children had formed a circled around Scott (picture vultures) in the church lobby. When I saw that, I purposely walked right past all of them. My oldest daughter, Taylor, grabbed my arm and said, "Mom! Where are you going?"

"I'm going to the bathroom."

"Mom, join the circle."

I thought to myself, "You guys are mine, and I don't want to be in the middle of that circle!"

Instead, I said, "I really need to use the bathroom."

Taylor followed me in, waited for me to finish and led me back out to the circle where they were interviewing and analyzing the Harley-Trucker (who I was starting to pity now).

Jesse, nineteen now, gave him one of those subtle but very clear messages about how he was the oldest and he was there to protect me and the children. I smiled and listened without interrupting. Scott received the message; I could tell by the smile on his face as he nodded in agreement. He looked at Jesse like he respected what he was saying and doing, and thought it was cute all at the same time. I felt the same way.

I determined that pulling him aside and having a private conversation wasn't going to happen with the vultures circling so close by, so I let it go. A few minutes later, I heard Jonah ask Scott for his phone number.

Since I had been so offended last week at the mere mention of him giving me his number, he loudly and repeatedly said, "Sure Jonah! You want my phone number, so you can call Nick? Absolutely! You can call Nick at any time. Here's my number so you can call Nick!"

I kind of giggled because he was trying so hard not to offend me again.

He said his goodbyes to the children and then he said to me, "I hope you have a really wonderful Mother's Day. You sure do deserve it. I'm sorry it's raining today."

My response surprised him, "Oh, don't apologize for the rain. I love the rain."

He said, "Really? So, the rain doesn't bother you at all?"

"No. In fact, this is the perfect day for rain. I'll have to explain why sometime."

'What? What am I saying? Why will I have to explain it to him? I don't have to tell him anything!'

I wondered why in the world I said that and, furthermore, why I wanted to pour my heart out to him and tell him how special the rain is to me.

We said our goodbyes and off he went. When we left the church, all eleven of the children gave me their thumbs-up of approval, saying he was so nice and the girls added, really cute.

"Mom, you should go for it!"

Why did everyone keep forgetting this guy's "lifestyle" problem?

I reminded them, "You guys, he's a Harley-Trucker! Conversation over."

We went home and the girls began preparing me a lovely Mother's Day meal. While they were cooking, I quietly asked Jonah for Scott's phone number. I figured if I couldn't get him alone at church for the "rules" talk, I could just call him. That way, I would have his full attention and no interruptions. It was actually perfect. I looked down at the bulletin from church that had his name and phone number on it. I looked at his handwriting and wondered what kind of man he really was. I dialed his number and when he answered, he was shocked to hear my voice on the other end of the phone.

"Hi, Scott. This is Kim. From church?"

"Oh! Kim. Oh, hi! Wow! Hi! How are you?"

"I'm fine, and, how are you?"

"I'm doing just fine. Wow! I'm so glad you called..."

He then proceeded to profusely apologize for offending me the previous week. And, when I say profusely, I mean for about ten minutes! In fact, he went so far as to tell me that he spent much of the week trying to figure out how to "un-offend" me without offending me any further. He explained that he wanted to get a hold of my phone number so that he could call me to apologize but quickly realized that it would promote him from offensive to stalker status! He went on to explain that he had no intention of being inappropriate or even of asking me out on a date. He simply thought we could go and hang out with our kids as two single parents, maybe enjoy the sun and get to know each other better. He explained to me that he is careful to start a friendship first before he considers dating someone, so he had no intention of making any kind of romantic advances in the parking lot that day.

> HE SPENT MUCH OF THE WEEK TRYING TO FIGURE OUT HOW TO "UN-OFFEND" ME.

I thanked him for explaining but told him that's not at all why I called. That took him by even greater surprise.

"It's not?" He asked, "Why did you call then?"

"Well, I meant to talk to you about something at church today, but it was clear by the reception you got from my children that I wasn't going to get you alone for two minutes. I thought I'd call you instead, since

FREE!

Jonah had your number, and explain something to you that is very, very important. Something you would have no way of knowing if I don't explain it."

More curious, he asked, "Okay. And what is that?"

"Well, at the risk of me sounding like the stalker now, I have to tell you . . . My kids are falling for you."

He kind of chuckled, "What? What do you mean?"

"Well, ever since that first Sunday in the parking lot when you were kind to them, they have decided that, not only are you nice enough for me to date, but last Sunday they announced that I should marry you! I know that might sound crazy but when I tell you what they've been through, it will make a lot of sense."

I went on to explain to him that my children hadn't seen their father in months, that they had essentially been abandoned by him and that, when he was in their lives, he was somewhat physically present but not emotionally. I explained that our marriage had ended with physical violence toward two of the children. I helped him to understand that my children were so starved for a father figure in their lives that they would give their hearts to a virtual stranger who simply brought them shark teeth in a church parking lot. I explained to him that if he wanted to be friends with my kids, that would be fine, but that I had rules.

I could "hear" his smile as he replied, "Oh, you have rules. Okay, what are they?"

"Yes, I do. I have two. Rule number one is this: You're friends with my kids to be friends with the kids . . . ONLY."

I didn't want him taking the back door in to get to me. My kids were not going to be a back door for anyone and I was only interested in a front door kind of guy.

"Okay, what's Rule number two?"

"Rule number two is: If you're friends with my kids, you're friends for life. No ships passing through the night for them – not on my watch."

He said, "Okay, I can live with both of those rules."

'Um, what?' was the thought, but out loud, I said, "You can?"

I was expecting him to turn tail and run, as my mom used to say, but instead, he agreed to the terms and then he said something even more surprising.

"You're going to have to help me with this."

I wondered how I was going to help him. What exactly did he mean that I was going to have to do anything? I don't like it when people tell me "I have to" do anything? What in the world was that supposed to mean?

I scaled back my emotion a little and tried to sound more "chill."

"What exactly do you mean?"

"Well, this whole thing about them dealing with addiction, right? I don't know a lot about that. I want to understand. I want to be careful. I want to be able to do things and say things that will help them and not hurt them."

Can we say he got my attention? This stranger from the church parking lot began to ask me questions like: What is it like to love someone with an addiction? How has that affected you? How has it affected the children? What can you do about it? How do you begin to heal and help your children to heal? He asked me about my faith. He asked me what I learned from all of it.

Forty-five minutes later, we were still on the phone and he asked me, "Where do you see yourself five years from now?"

That was a loaded question and a great opportunity to see if he could be scared off. Oh, how I wanted to scare him off! I really wanted to answer him, but there was a knock on my bedroom door.

It was my daughter. "Mom, your Mother's Day lunch is ready."

I told Scott I would like to answer his question, but I could not talk anymore. I explained that lunch was waiting and so were my eleven dates and asked if I could call him later to finish our conversation.

He said, "Of course. Absolutely."

We both said it was nice chatting and we hung up. The kids were surprised to learn that I just hung up the phone with the Harley-Trucker guy. As we sat down to the meal, I could not believe I talked with a stranger for forty-five minutes and was even more shocked by how much I enjoyed it! I scarfed my food down in minutes and sat and waited for my kids to eat. I wanted to call him back!

I explained to the kids that he had asked me a question that I wanted to answer and asked if they would mind if I went to my room and called him back. The little matchmakers grabbed me by the arm, led me to my room, pushed me inside and closed the door! I dialed his number again and this time when he heard my voice he was laughing.

He answered saying, "Oh! When you said later, I didn't think you meant ten minutes!"

I felt a little silly and I guess it was kind of soon to be considered later, but I didn't care. I hadn't had that engaging a conversation with a man . . . ever. He was at Walmart when I called the first time and was still there the second time, but didn't seem to mind talking. We continued our conversation and, two hours later, after he put his milk back in the cooler three separate times, we got off the phone. I came out of the bedroom and I couldn't believe what just happened.

We connected on so many levels. We had the same sense of humor, the same favorite movie, the same love for good conversation. I thought I might have finally found someone who talked more than me! (I was right.) He applauded my goals, my dreams, and vision for my destiny. In fact, when I told him my five-year plan in hopes of scaring him off, the opposite happened. I even beefed up my answer! I told him that in five years I saw myself speaking, writing, traveling around the country and world, and changing it, one heart at a time if necessary.

I was pleasantly surprised by his response.

"Oh, wow, that's great! I will be right there in the back row cheering you on."

At first, I thought that was some pretty wishful thinking.

I laughed and said, "What? Why the back row?"

"Well," he confessed, "I can't stand being the center of attention! If I had to do what you want to do, I'd drop right there on the stage and you'd have to bring out the paddles and shock my heart. Clear!"

I laughed at the thought of that scene and I found it interesting how different he was from me.

He went on, "That's really great for you. Wow. Good for you, you have a huge heart! But seriously, that is not for me. Not my dream. At all. But I'll be happy to cheer you on!"

He applauded my vision and my passion and wasn't the least bit intimidated by it. I couldn't scare him off with our "Jerry Springer" story so I tried to do it with my plan to change the world. Neither worked. I guess if eleven kids, years of alcoholism and co-dependency didn't scare him off, a big destiny wouldn't either. Scott's concern for my family proved to be genuine and our friendship began.

We began texting later that evening and he made me laugh like I had not laughed in eighteen years . . . maybe longer. By the end of that first week, he was at my house repairing my lawn mower, so he could mow my lawn for me. Even after his hard work, new tires, and a whole evening spent on repairing it, it died. So, the next time he came to do my lawn, he rolled into the driveway with a trailer on the back of his vehicle with a new riding lawnmower fastened to it.

I said, "What in the world is that?"

"I bought this so I can cut your grass!"

I was stunned. He took care of me. He took care of the house. He took care of things that were broken. He took care of hearts that were broken. He took Maci, who was nine-years-old, to Fleet Farm with him to buy those tractor tires that first night he came over. He asked her what her mom's favorite treat was. She came home and proudly handed me a bag of chocolate-covered peanuts. That's when I knew I was in for trouble.

Not that I was totally trusting. I wasn't. I was intrigued, but very skeptical. It's funny because, after answering a number of his questions about me and who I was, my first question for him during that first Mother's Day call was, "So, when's the last time you used drugs or alcohol?"

Yes, I was that bold (rude). His response caught me off guard. I expected a smoke screen of some sort. Excuses. Instead, I got what I've come to expect from him now, a typical dose of his sense of humor with the truth between the lines.

"Well, I'll be honest. All those years I spent alone, I told myself so many times, *'Self, this would be a lot easier if you picked up a drug habit,'* but I never got around to it. I just kept working and spending time with my son."

I couldn't help but to laugh at his funny answer. It was serious, too, and I believed him. He went on to tell me he was tempted like anyone else to forget his pain and drown his sorrows, but chose instead to stay out of the bars, to work hard and be the best dad he could be to his son.

'Is he telling me what every woman wants to hear or is he really that good?'

Luckily, I knew a lot of people from church who knew him a lot longer than I did. I did my homework and found out that he had not, in fact, picked up a drug habit. Actually, I had more skeletons in my closet than he ever did. He wasn't a drinker, wasn't a smoker, and never did a drug in his life. This former home-schooling mom of eleven had a more speckled past than the Harley-Trucker that I had stereotyped and rejected before I gave him a chance. I've learned a lot of lessons since I've met Scott . . . even more since I've loved him. (Yes, that part is coming! Hold on!) I'm so thankful that he proved me wrong.

We decided to be friends, but our friendship didn't last long. It quickly turned into love as we talked about everything from our past to our future, from our hopes to our dreams, from our favorite movies to our favorite foods – you name it. He continued to serve my family and was there for me when I needed him. I watched him raise his son. He was an incredible father, and he still is. He adored his son like I've never seen any father adore his son. They spent every moment together that they could. They worked together, played together, and they traveled together. He knew everything about his son, talked of him with pride, and was kind and gentle toward him. I was blown away.

At the same time, he was kind and gentle toward me and toward my children. As our feelings became more intense, we decided we needed to talk to the kids.

One day, I called a family meeting with the kids, Scott, and me. All eleven were there, and seated, so I collected everyone's cell phones and devices and put them in a basket. With their full attention, I told them I had an announcement to make.

"What is it?" they asked reluctantly.

"Well," I explained, "You know how I told you that Scott and I were just going to be friends? We want you kids to know that we are no longer going to be friends."

Their faces looked surprised and shocked as I finished the statement by saying, "We are going to be more than friends! We want to be boyfriend and girlfriend."

Several of the little kids smiled from ear to ear and buried their faces in pillows out of embarrassment and excitement. Everybody was happy for me, even some of the older, less trusting, more skeptical kids.

Scott took time to carefully explain that he wasn't trying to take anyone's place, especially their dad's. He told them that he could be to each of them what they wanted him to be. A friend maybe. Or someone to talk to. Maybe more. Or maybe nothing at all. He told them that it was up to each of them to decide. He assured them that if they had any questions, they could go ahead and ask, and he would do his best to answer.

Jesse was the first to speak. "I have a question. Are you blind?"

After we all were done laughing, Scott replied, "No, I'm not blind. What do you mean?"

FREE!

Jesse said, "Look around. Look around you. My mom has eleven kids. Do you know what you're getting yourself into?"

Scott smiled and replied, "Yes, I'm aware that your mom has eleven kids and, although I've never had eleven kids myself, I am very okay with that."

Jesse said, "Yeah, but aren't you scared?"

Scott said, "I'm sure there will be times when I am scared. Maybe a lot of times. But I'm not scared right now. No."

Then fifteen-year-old Alex got right to the point. (He takes after his mother.) "Scott, do you drink?"

Scott's response was sincere and honest – true to form – as he said, "You know, I was on a bike trip recently out to Washington D.C. and some of the guys gave me a beer when I was out there. I took it to be polite, but I didn't drink it. I just don't like the taste of alcohol. I don't drink."

Alex scoffed silently and his eyes said, 'We'll see.'

Time has proven that Scott is a truthful man. From that moment forward, we were madly in love, inseparable, and on a roller-coaster ride of love, joy and delight. He was there for me when I laughed. He was there to make me laugh! He was there for me when I cried. He was there to pray for me, talk me off several ledges, reassure me, encourage me, and hold my hand. He helped me with the kids. He helped me with the bills. He took me places I had never been. He woke me in the morning with loving texts and said good-night to me at night with the same. He constantly surprised me with things that he knew would bring me joy. He told me I was beautiful all the time. He saw the good in me. He treated me like a queen. I couldn't believe the love I was experiencing.

During that time of my Esther fast, God told me that he was going to bring an extravagant love into my life. I knew God's love was extravagant; I had experienced that. But, I had never been loved extravagantly by a man – until Scott loved me.

Over the course of the next two years, I discovered that this love that I was so desperate for, that I had waited so long for, and that I prayed for and fully believed God had brought to me was more than a blessing. It was also a distraction in my life. A really big one.

I found that I spent less time with the Lord and more time with Scott. I stopped writing and journaling altogether which had been a huge part of my walk with God for the previous fifteen years. I discovered that I didn't have as much interest in going to church as I used to. Oh sure, I went occasionally, but my heart wasn't the same when I was there and this bothered me. What bothered me more was that I didn't want to do anything about it. My heart was devoted to a man and, for a time, I was really okay with that. He was filling my tank, I was filling his, and I was living my dream. He was living to make my dreams come true and it was working. Over time, though, it bothered me more and more. I knew God wasn't the center of our relationship. I lived for "us" and "we"—not for Him.

I would raise my concerns to Scott at times and he would say, "What do you mean? We both love God. He's at the center. We go to church. We pray together."

I couldn't argue with that. Those things were true. So, I would quiet myself for a while, until it would begin to bother me again. At about the two-year mark, we were running into trouble. This underlying battle over who sat on the throne of my heart just wouldn't let go of me. I was torn. It also bothered me that we were together two years and there was not a ring on my finger. I knew that he loved me, but I didn't know what his intentions were and, it bothered me that I had to wonder. Was I selling out? Or worse . . . was I selling out just to end up alone again? Would my children be left high and dry - again?

This led to some difficulty and conflict, but the real issue, the underlying issue was that deep down: I knew that the man God chose for me would not be the man that is content with sitting on the throne of my life. He would be the man that insisted that God be on the throne of my life.

Not that it was Scott's fault that I put him on the throne. It wasn't. I take full responsibility for that. I thought that I had been healed of so many wounds from my first marriage. I felt like a secure woman when I met Scott, but feelings can be deceitful. I had learned to love in a really hard but righteous way, but I was still insecure. I didn't know how to get my security from the Lord. I always tried to find it in a man and, when I had that security from God in my marriage, it was because there was no man there to offer it to me. But now there was. There was a man who loved me so thoroughly, so completely, and so wholeheartedly that I allowed that to be the source of my emotional security.

The day came when that would not do anymore. God told me that if I stayed on the path I was on, I would not fulfill my destiny. I knew exactly what He meant. It is what I had been secretly fearing.

> LOVE WAS GOOD. LIFE WAS GOOD. BUT WAS IT THE BEST?

I thought that God gave me Scott – that Scott was the answer to my prayers. But how could that could be true if staying with him would take me off the path to my destiny? I knew the road I was on with Scott was to something good. Love was good. Life was good. But was it the best?

If God's best for me was to love and be loved and fulfill my destiny, then I wasn't going to make it there if I kept this man in my life. I was too broken to choose God over Scott and keep Scott around. I kept slipping God off the throne and putting Scott back on. God would have given us a good life, but I didn't fight, cry, pray, and believe for two decades for something "good." I wanted it all. Remember? That is what I asked for. Sometimes good is the enemy of best and, in this case, I knew it was.

Almost exactly two years after we met, I called him, and I told him, "I cannot be with you anymore."

He asked me why.

"If I try to explain it to you, I know that you will talk me out of it. It's going to be hard enough for me to do this and to stick to it, without you talking me out of it. So please don't ask for an explanation. Please don't try to talk me out of it. And please know that I love you and I will always love you in some way—but I have to do this. I have to say goodbye."

I told him it would be best if we didn't speak at all and I would have his things delivered to his house. A week later, some mutual friends came over with a trailer. I knew these friends would faithfully deliver everything that I had of Scott's—the lawnmower, all kinds of household items, furniture, and his car—to him. He had given me his car to drive several weeks after we met and I had driven it for two years. I sold my big red fifteen passenger van before it broke down and relied fully on his car. So, when I returned his car, I knew I'd be left with no vehicle, but I needed to cut the ties completely.

I knew that if I had his car, I would have to talk to him and I knew that if I had his car, he would have a reason to talk to me. I knew, if a little light went on in the dashboard or it made the wrong noise, I would be back in his arms again in no time. I couldn't risk it. My heart was broken – saying good-bye to him, saying good-bye to our love, saying good-bye to the best thing I had ever known in my life. But God told me that He was all I needed. So, I expected Him to provide all that we'd need.

Scott was crushed. He wasn't ready to say goodbye. He continued to reach out to the children, but I knew that they wouldn't heal if they still had him in their life. I knew that sometimes you have to make a clean break. Sometimes, to save the body, you have to chop off the leg and I knew that this was one of those times. I explained to my children that he couldn't be in my life anymore because I was going to miss my destiny if I stayed with him. I told the kids that I put Scott before God in my heart and that nothing in the world was worth missing my destiny and not living my truest purpose, no matter how good it is. I told them that I knew it was hard for them to understand and I was so sorry for breaking their little hearts again.

I went on to say, "Since he can't be in our lives, then it's just prolonging the pain to keep talking to him, even if it is only with text messages and phone calls. I can't allow him to spend time with you. I can't allow him in my life. I'm so sorry for how painful this is for all of us, but we have to say good-bye for once and for all."

I asked him to please stop contacting the kids.

Well, as if the first blow wasn't enough, this one crushed him to the core. His heart ached as he missed not one, not two, but twelve people and the dream in his heart of a family that he thought was being fulfilled.

As that summer went on without him, we had incredible highs and some real obstacles to overcome. First of all, I didn't have a vehicle and I had to get to work to support my family. I was still cleaning houses. I had given up all my other jobs and decided I would work on my terms and on my terms only to be available for my children when they needed me. I began to take

FREE!

better care of myself and give more time and attention to my health, more time and attention to my kids, and a lot more time and attention to the Lord. I dove in to the Word of God again. I began to experience His presence like I did during those days of the Esther fast before I met Scott. I looked forward to every evening when I could be alone with the Lord. He gave me revelation upon revelation and truth upon truth. He gave me such a huge vision for my life I could hardly contain it. He told me I was on the brink of crossing over that Jordan River into my Promised Land. I knew that, for whatever reason I had to say good-bye to Scott, I had done the right thing. I knew that decision catapulted me to a new place in the Kingdom and a new place with my God.

My children watched and marveled.

My daughter Kelsey told me later, "Mom, that summer is my foremost memory of you growing up. You were the most fearless, the most joyful, and the most amazing. Nothing scared you. You were always happy, even though we had the least during those days."

> YOU WERE THE MOST FEARLESS, THE MOST JOYFUL, AND THE MOST AMAZING.

I love how God uses a mess to broadcast his message. During those days, my Maker truly was my Husband. I don't regret a single moment of any of it. Have I mentioned before in this book that I don't live with regrets? Why should I have to? If I serve a God who works all things together for my good, then why bother living with regrets? I don't believe you can do both. Either you trust Him to work everything together for good or you sit around and regret it. I choose trust. I choose to smile when I think of my highs, my lows, my successes and my failures. I don't consider my two years with Scott a failure; I consider them a massive success. Why? Because they weren't wasted. Because I am the woman I am today because God brought a love into my life that revealed an insecurity in me that ran so deep that it took a massive action to heal me. I love the well-known saying that God loves you just the way you are but loves you too much to leave you that way. That's what he did for me by revealing my wound and insecurity. He gave me the opportunity to heal. By saying, "no" to that idol in my life, "no" to that false security, "no" to the wrong king on the right throne, I stepped into a new place emotionally and spiritually.

During the six months that followed my breakup with Scott, God started to speak to me about my future husband. He began to prepare me for the marriage that He willed for my life. He spoke to me about Rebecca and Isaac of the Old Testament. He showed me how Rebecca was going about her business and doing what was right when the servant of Abraham came and chose her and told her that she was to be the bride of Isaac.

God assured me that, like in this story, I would marry my Isaac. After the servant of Abraham chose Rebecca, he led her to where she would become Isaac's bride. Isaac was out in the field when he saw her being led by the servant on a camel. I pictured myself being led on a camel to my Isaac. Just like Rebecca, I didn't know who or where he was. I also didn't know when I would stumble upon him, but I did believe I was on my way.

It's funny how many women ask me, "Weren't you afraid you wouldn't find love again because of how many kids you had?"

I never once doubted that I would find love again. I never once doubted that I wouldn't get my prayers answered. Remember the Golden Scepter? Once you've touched it, you'll never doubt again. I was alone again, but I wasn't doubting. I knew that my Isaac was out there and that I was his Rebecca.

One day, Sue called me and said, "Kim! The camels are moving!" I laughed. Sue had a prophetic message for me that I didn't understand at first.

"There are camels on a farm that I pass on the way to my house. Every day, I drive past the camels and they're standing still. I have never, ever seen them moving. Today, they were moving, and God said it was a sign for you. The camels are on the move."

She didn't even know what it meant, but I did! God was leading me to my Isaac! (God brought Rebecca to her husband Isaac on a camel.) Over the course of the next few months, I waited and prayed. One day, while cleaning a house, I got a text message. It was from Scott.

"Thank you," was all it said.

I looked down at my phone and I began to shake. It had been months since I had heard from him or he heard from me. Thank you? What does he mean by that?

Was it sarcastic? For some reason, I was up for a fight, so I decided I would call him and find out. I dialed his number.

When he answered, I simply said, "What is that supposed to mean?"

He said with kindness in his voice, "Oh, I just can't help but to be so thankful. I'm just driving along thanking God for you. Thanking God that I had you and your kids in my life. Even if it was just two short years. *They were the best two years of my life.* So many good things, so many good memories and, as I'm driving along, I'm just thanking God and so I decided to thank you, too. That's all."

Well, as you probably already predicted, that conversation led to another, which led to another and, as I stated earlier, within twenty-four hours, we were together again. Not back together, but together talking, together laughing, together seeing a movie, together walking around, together driving around and, by the weekend, we were holding hands. I found myself walking along the lakefront in Milwaukee looking at beautiful Lake Michigan with the love of my life after many long months of being apart, knowing that I still could not be with him. We sat down on a bench with the beautiful scenery laid out in front of us and the beautiful love that we both so desperately missed between us. He held me, and he kissed me, and he whispered in my ear the words I longed to hear him say since the moment I fell in love with him.

He asked me to be his wife.

'*Why now?*' I thought. "You know I can't do that."

He said, "I know you think you can't."

"No, I know I can't," I argued, "And you know, as much as I want to say yes, I can't. No matter how wonderful all this feels right now, when it's over, we are going to have to have a conversation that you are not going to like."

He said, "I'll take my chances."

"You know, you really shouldn't be with me at all right now," I advised him. "Actually, if you were smart, you would get up and run to your car right now because you know this is not going to end well. You know I'm going to have to break your heart again."

"It's worth the risk in my opinion," he said with a smile.

"Why would you keep subjecting yourself to more pain?" I asked.

"Don't worry about me, Kim, I'll take care of myself. And besides, God's got me."

We continued laughing, talking, and holding hands. I went home late that night in a dichotomy. I loved being with him again. His smell and his laugh and his touch. No one else has his kind eyes. No one. No one was like him and no one could make me feel like he did. And then came the but . . . BUT I can't be with him. No matter how good, it's not what's best. I cannot miss my destiny for

I CANNOT MISS MY DESTINY FOR ANYONE.

anyone. I can't. I've already given up so much. I've already suffered so much. I wanted God's absolute best for me and my kids. I had to change other people's lives, not just my own. I reasoned that, if Scott was not "the one," then whoever he was, he must be second only to Jesus Himself! I knew what I had to do.

Scott called me the next day. He was full of love, full of promise. He told me God had given him a sign. He saw not one, not two, but multiple hot air balloons in the sky that day. He explained how a hot air balloon represented me to him.

"They are beautiful, and captivating, and they just gracefully float along, all the while taking people higher. They are just like you, Kim." He explained that this is precisely why, when we were dating, he had contemplated proposing to me in a hot air balloon. Again, with the marriage talk! Why couldn't he have talked like this a year ago?

HE WAS SO MOVED BY WHAT HE SAW AND FELT. SO HOPEFUL. SO ELATED. IT WAS A SPECIAL MOMENT BETWEEN HIM AND GOD.

He went on to tell me that he believed that the balloons were a sign from God that he would be with me again. That we were meant to be together. That I would in fact be his wife someday. He was so moved by what he saw and felt. So hopeful. So elated. It was a special moment between him and God.

On the other end of the phone, I couldn't help but to feel bad for him. I thought about how sad it was for him that he thought his own wishful thinking was actually God giving him hope. My heart broke because I knew I had to crush his dream again. I reasoned that keeping his hope alive would be cruel to us both.

The next morning, my soul was in a vice grip. As much as I wanted to, I knew I could not continue this relationship. I knew that I had to break free from Scott's love in order to fulfill my destiny. Two nights earlier that very love was handed to me on a silver platter in the form of a marriage proposal. I had to say no. I dialed the phone to say one final goodbye.

He asked why I called.

I paused for what seemed like an eternity and finally mustered it up. "I'm so sorry. I cannot be with you."

I recalled it all at my eighth grave; the place where I sacrificed.

Scott didn't understand. He didn't agree. He continued to try to change my mind. This conversation was more difficult for him than the first, but my resolve was strengthening.

I did this once before; I could do it again. I empathized with him, I really did. My heart broke for him, but I had to ask him not to contact me. I told him it was obvious that we could never just be friends.

He texted me a while later. I knew that this could go on and on. I felt that for both of our sakes, I had no choice but to block him from my cell phone. This final blow crushed him to the core, but I had to do it. He was the drug I was addicted to and I had to go cold turkey. It was time to move forward with God. I had come too far these last months. I wasn't willing to throw it away.

Two months later, I stood at his doorstep. God orchestrated my steps. It was the equivalent of Abraham's servant putting Rebecca on a camel and leading her to Isaac. As I stood at his door and knocked, I had no idea what God was doing. I thought I knew what I was doing. I stood at the door and wondered what kind of reception I was going to get. Part of me thought that he might slam the door in my face, with good reason. Most of me still believed he would never do that. Well, most of me was right. He opened the door and welcomed me with open arms. At first, he was sure an accident or emergency had happened with me or one of the kids for me to be at his house. He asked question after question to investigate. I assured him we were all well. He asked about our safety, our health, or did I need money? He asked if I was having car troubles. He asked if I was sick. Like, really sick. No, I promised, it was none of those things.

Once he was convinced there was no problem he sat me down and showed me gracious hospitality. He offered me a drink, gave me a blanket, put a heater by my feet because it was a cold evening and he knows I'm always cold. He asked me what else he could do for me. I told him there was nothing else I needed. But once I was there, looking directly into his kind eyes, I couldn't bring myself to hurt him again. I just couldn't tell him. We sat in silence.

He asked, "Do you want to talk?"

"No."

"Do you want to go get something to eat?"

"No."

"Do you want to watch some TV?"

"Sure." I said. We sat and watched TV for a little while and I asked him if I could lean on his chest.

He said, "Sure."

I nestled my head in, closed my eyes, pinched myself a little bit to make sure this was real. Although I still believed I couldn't be with him forever, I felt no guilt being there with him. I looked up at him and I asked him to kiss me.

Turning his head in the other direction he said, "Oh no, no, no."

What? He never said no to me!

See that chair over there?" He pointed to his recliner.

I said, "Yes."

He went on, "Well, we're over here on this couch and Jesus is right there in my chair. And He's with us and watching us. And I won't kiss you in front of Him until you know that you can be my wife. Until you say that you'll be mine forever, I won't kiss you."

I don't like to be told no. I prefer to get my way and I wasn't used to being told no by him. I wasn't happy that he wouldn't kiss me, but boy, was I intrigued! What did he mean he wouldn't kiss me until I said I would be his wife? Why is it, after everything we've been through that he's still holding on to the belief that I will be Mrs. Krueger some day? (Ahem! I hear you laughing over there. Yes, I know what the name on the cover of this book is!) I couldn't believe my ears. Where did his confidence come from? I stayed a little longer and then went home with a warm hug.

The next day I called him.

"I did come over for a reason last night."

"I know you did."

"You do?"

"Yes. And I know what the reason is, too."

"You do? What was my reason, then?"

Scott always had this way of reading my mind. In fact, he read my mind the first time he saw me after our phone friendship began. He could see my heart right through my eyes. Apparently, he could even do it over the phone.

"You came over here last night to tell me that you're getting ready to move on with some other guy. I'm not a fool, Kim."

He was right, and I was stunned. How in the world did he know that? Crazy! A man that I had met was getting ready to ask me on a date. I was going to tell Scott so that he would finally let me go for good. Then I could finally let him go, too. Great plan, right?

He went on, "It's all good. You found some guy that makes you happy or whatever, that's great. I just have one question for you."

I braced myself and asked, "What is it?"

"If he's so great, and he's all that, what were you doing in my arms last night?"

It takes a lot to make this girl speechless. No man does it as well as this one. Just as if a warm front collided with a cold front, a severe thunderstorm developed on the inside me. He was right. He was so right. What was I doing in his arms last night?

What was I doing back in his house? Why did I have to tell him anything about what I was doing? I didn't have to, so why did I? And what was I doing thinking about beginning a relationship with anyone else while my heart clearly belonged to this mind-reading, adoring, Harley-Trucker? I was a mess inside. But one thing was for certain. The other guy would never do. Nothing personal . . . he just wasn't Scott.

The next morning, crying my eyes out, I called Scott and said, "Where are you? I need to see you right now." I told him that my heart was a mess. I wanted to be with him more than life itself, but I still didn't think I could. Nevertheless, I missed him more than anything in the world. I told him how much of a struggle it was to go on without him, how I ached inside for so long and never could have done it if it wasn't my destiny at stake. I was such a mess inside again and I needed to see him.

He told me where he was and said he would wait there for me. He talked me through my breakdown for the whole forty-minute drive. It is amazing what he's endured in the name of his love for me.

When I arrived, he took me by the hand and he told me, "Kim, I know why I lost you and the kids."

"You do?"

"Yes. Why?"

"I lost you because I didn't point you and the kids to Jesus. Kim, of all of the people in the world who need the Lord, it's you and it's your children. I should have been faithful, and I should have pointed you to God all along, not to me. That's why I lost you. What was I thinking?"

He asked himself with tears in his eyes, now falling onto my leg as he stood over me.

"But I promise you this," he went on, "if I ever have the opportunity to be in your lives again, I will not make that mistake twice."

I could not believe my ears. I couldn't believe that he was finally agreeing with what I had been saying all along. Our time apart also showed him that his priorities weren't in the right place, and he was apologizing to me for the choices he made. I never thought that day would come and I treasured it.

I wondered, *'What in the world is God doing?'*

Later that same day I said, "How would you like to see the kids tonight?"

FREE!

He said, "What? Are you sure? I don't know. Are you sure you want me to see them? You didn't want me to see them."

I said, "Yes! They would love to see you!" All hesitation was gone, and I felt totally free to invite him over to see the kids, but I didn't tell them. We surprised them that evening. When the kids got home from school that afternoon, I told them we were going to have a special visitor after dinner.

"Who? Who?" They asked with anticipation.

"It's a surprise!"

They scurried around to get their chores and homework done and waited. They heard a motorcycle pull into the driveway but didn't think for a minute it would be Scott. They were so confused about who would be driving up on a motorcycle. They made a few guesses – none of which were Scott.

By the time he got up to the window where they could see him, they said, "No way! It is Scott!!"

They ran outside to greet him. It was pure joy! Even Kelsey, my seventeen-year-old who was eating dinner threw down her fork and ran outside to hug him.

That evening, I also welcomed him to come back to church where we met. He had stopped going to that church after we broke up so that the kids and I could remain there. He did come back to church the following week and attended with me. I also told Lynda and Sue what was happening. I told them about my questions about what God was doing.

And then, I secretly and quietly prayed a prayer of guidance, telling no one:

Lord, you know I don't trust myself when it comes to my feelings for this man. You know how much I love him. You know how hard it was for me to say good-bye to him. I am absolutely and positively ready to do whatever you tell me to do when it comes to him. If this is you – if it is you bringing us back together, if he is in fact, my Isaac, then have all eleven of my kids, my two mentors and my pastor and his wife give me their blessing to marry him. That's fifteen blessings Lord. I need to know that everybody in my life sees that this is your hand, not just my emotions. Amen.

Over the course of the next two weeks, all eleven of my kids, both of my spiritual mothers, and both of my pastors all said the same thing.

"This is God."

"This is God."

"God has done a work in you and God has done a work in him."

Pastor Sue came up to me one day in church, grabbed my hand, and said, "Kim. The Lord has brought you to your Isaac."

She had no idea about the camel, no idea about the verses regarding Rebecca and Isaac that I had read, no idea about my prayer! I began to understand that I had been tested. Just like Abraham had received his promise in the form of Isaac, his son, and was asked to sacrifice him, so was I. Abraham had to take his Isaac up to Mt. Horeb, lay him on the altar, bind his hands and feet and prepare to sacrifice him to God and so did I.

The Lord said clearly to me, "You have passed the test and you can have your Isaac back" just like he did to Abraham.

I couldn't wait to tell him that he could finally kiss me! Actually, I couldn't wait to not get turned down again! That man would not kiss me for anything! He stuck to his guns on that one. We were sitting at his home one night having dinner that he had prepared – well, prepared is a stretch – he ordered it.

We were eating quietly when I looked up at him and casually announced between bites, "Oh, by the way, you can kiss me tonight."

He was getting so used to me trying to get him to kiss me, that he said, "Now Kim, you know I can't do that."

I put my fork down, smiled and I said, "No. I mean... *You can FINALLY kiss me tonight.*"

He looked at me with a little sparkle in his eye as he began to smile, indicating that he understood. He ate the rest of his dinner with that grin on his face that I had come to adore because I knew that thoughts of me were behind it. Eventually, we cleaned up our meal and He took me by the hands. He pledged his love to me, pledged his heart to me, he betrothed himself to me with the most beautiful words I had ever heard in my life. He said his vows to me.

Then he kissed me.

The only way I can explain it is that I was kissed with the best kiss that has ever been kissed in the history of kissing. That kiss meant we would be husband and wife. That kiss was not just a promise, it was a commitment.

It was so worth the wait. I was glad that he didn't listen to me and that he wouldn't kiss me until I knew I could be his wife.

I am his wife and have been his wife now for over seven years. I'm so thankful that the Lord gave me my heart's desire and then asked me to sacrifice it. I would do it all over again in a heartbeat. When God asks you to do something crazy, just do it. When God asks you to do something hard, just do it. When God asks you to take the high road, make the sacrifice, forgive, trust, move on, start over, step out . . . just do it! It is so worth it!

As I sat at Lake Michigan on the last day of the Feast of Tabernacles looking at that eighth beautiful, heart-breaking, grave, the place where I sacrificed my lifelong dream to love and be loved, I didn't know yet that God was going to bring Scott back into my life. I was convinced that the chapter on Scott and Kim was written and closed.

I sat in my car on that beautiful fall day looking at the bench where he asked me to be his wife, where he pledged his love to me, where I said no to my dream and I heard the voice of my Father say, "I'm so proud of you. I'm so proud of you. *You gave it all up for Me.*"

Even believing I would never see Scott again, the Lord's words made it all worthwhile. I shed what I thought would be my last tear for that sacrifice. I looked at that place on Lake Michigan as a mountaintop where I built an altar to the Lord and sacrificed my promise and I drove away with the peace and joy that comes from obedience.

Once home, I collected my notebook, Bible, tissues, and pen and I marvelled at the week I had spent dancing on graves. I had a pure heart. I had a whole heart. I had a heart healed from abandonment, a hardened, angry heart that learned to forgive, a broken heart that learned to dance, a heart healed of abuse and its scars of shame. I now had a heart that was healed from being orphaned and alone. I was no longer lonely, even though I was alone. I had a heart that was healed from persecution and public shame. I had a heart that no longer feared failure, but embraced the mistakes it made and loved itself in spite of them. I had a heart that overcame addictions and learned how to love those who haven't overcome their addictions. I had a heart that I now knew was willing to sacrifice the thing it longed for and waited for the most.

Epilogue

I won't hold out on you; I promise. I will tell you how my love story ended. Actually, I will tell you about its new beginning. After all, the number eight represents new beginnings, so it was no mistake that grave number eight wasn't a grave after all.

On November 11, 2010, Scott, the kids, and I were reunited by the Holy Spirit in tears and joy. Shortly after that, I got the green light from God to marry him and he kissed me with "that kiss." One month later, on December 11 –just three months after my grave-visiting journey ended, Scott flew me to Florida and proposed to me. He chose a beautiful place called Stump Pass Beach, specifically because it was an opening from a narrow channel of water to the endless and glorious Gulf of Mexico. He said he wanted his love to be that for me, an opening from a narrow place to a wide-open place of endless possibilities. He got down on one knee on the beach and asked me to be his wife.

I tearfully and ecstatically said, "Yes!"

FREE!

One month later, on 1/11/11, we were married at a venue located right on the Milwaukee Lakefront . . . where I *sacrificed* my promise of love in obedience to God.

Doesn't God write the BEST stories? I didn't only dance on the last grave, I married a dance partner I could take out on God's dance floor for the rest of my days in this life.

Oh, and about all of the elevens; I guess I forgot to tell you what the number eleven has come to mean to me. Do you remember those infamous Mother's Day phone calls? They happened on May 11, which is my mom's birthday. I had raised eleven children (before happily becoming stepmom to a twelfth). Scott and I were engaged on the 11th and married on the 11th.

Every time I see the number eleven, I smile at God . . . because it is God's way of smiling at me. It is His special way of telling me that I am blessed beyond blessed. Even the proposal I said no to at that beautiful Lakefront "grave" happened on September 11th, bringing joy to a date that makes so many think of ashes. Eleven has come to represent the greatest blessings in my life.

True to form, the year 2011 did not disappoint. It brought many new blessings – a new marriage, a new life, a new home, a new town, and a new calling.

In 2011, I began writing the book that you're reading today. 2011 is also the year that God opened the door for me to live my purpose as author, publisher, and speaker.

With Jesus on the throne of my heart, never to be replaced, and Scott by my side, I am fulfilling my God-given purpose every day. The graves of my past that Satan meant to be *setbacks*, God turned into a *set-up* for my destiny!

What do your graves look like? Having them does not disqualify you from making a significant impact on the world; rather, they may qualify you toward your purpose.

It is only in not being healed by God that your graves will hinder you. Allowing God to take you grave-dancing is the way that you can become an answer to the world.

And the world needs you to be an answer!

The world needs you to overcome the deaths of your past with Jesus . . . and tell your story.

That's what The Promised Land is all about. It isn't just a place of blessing and abundance to be enjoyed, although that is part of it. It is also a place where we get to take back the ground the enemy has stolen from us and God's other children. It is the place where we "overcome by the blood of the Lamb and the Word of our testimony," – *our testimony of God's Faithfulness in our Wilderness.*

If there is one prevailing theme in all of these chapters, it is that God did not waste one moment of my suffering, sorrow, loss, pain, failure, or sacrifice. He didn't waste my Wilderness. And He won't waste yours either.

God is inviting you to your own personal "Festival of Tabernacles" – your own healing journey. He wants you to remember His Goodness and His Faithfulness to you during those dry and lonely days. He longs to show you where He was when those graves were being dug.

God is inviting you to visit your graves with Him... and be FREE!

About the Author

Kimberly
Joy
Krueger

Kimberly Krueger has overcome some of life's toughest struggles with beauty, dignity and grace; with her eyes looking up and never looking back.

She fell in love with running in 2014and has since run over ten 5Ks, half and full marathons. After being hit by a car in 2014, she ran a half marathon just eleven months later. Her favorite race to run, though, is her race with God; and she runs it to WIN!

As a third-generation entrepreneur, she has set her goals set high and continues to reach higher while helping women to see their true value and reach their God-given potential. Her mission is to empower women to live extraordinary lives and tell their stories.

Through The Fellowship of Extraordinary Women (FEW) monthly meetings, FEW's Women's Leadership Course, and FEW International Publications, she is doing just that—by leaps and bounds.

Kimberly says that her greatest accomplishment in life is being a wife to Scott, mother to twelve children and "Noni" to five perfect grandchildren. Her closest friends will tell you that she is "a mom to many and a friend to all." For fun, she transforms into a 'Biker Chic," and rides alongside her husband, Scott, on *her* Harley-Davidson® Road King.

Learn more at www.kimberlyjoykrueger.com.

Scott & Kim

January 11, 2011

From Left to Right: Ava, Ella, Maci, Kelsey, Taylor, Kimberly, Scott, Jesse, Alex, Jake, Jonah, Nick, Isaac and Eli

Acknowledgments

I'd like to offer my sincerest thanks to Reji Laberje, FEW Coach, editor, and friend. Reji, you not only enriched this book with your expertise and experience, but you freely committed yourself to spreading its message. Most of all, I am grateful for your belief in me and the call that God has placed on my life!

To my loving husband and twelve extraordinary children: No one has been more important to the telling of my story than you. You have loved me and believed in me through all eight graves and yet, remain! I adore you!

Above all, my most humble gratitude is reserved for my Heavenly Father, my Lord and Savior, Jesus Christ, and The Comforter; You have truly turned my mourning into dancing!

Printed in the United States of America

Made in the USA
Middletown, DE
28 May 2022

66346540R00109